from the wrong side

a paradoxical approach to psychology

Adolf Guggenbühl-Craig

**With a Commentary on the Work and Thought of
Adolf Guggenbühl-Craig
by Sidney Handel**

**Edited and Translated from the German
by Gary V. Hartman**

SPRING PUBLICATIONS
Woodstock, Connecticut

SPRING PUBLICATIONS, INC.
299 EAST QUASSETT ROAD
WOODSTOCK, CONNECTICUT 06281

Distributed in the United Stated by the Continuum Publishing Group; in Canada by McClelland & Stewart; in the United Kingdom, Eire and Europe by Airlift Book Co.; and in Austrailia by Astam Books Pty Ltd.

ISBN 0-88214-357-3

CONTENTS

Editor's Foreword

   This book began life as *Vom Guten des Boesen* (*On Evil's Good*), the title of the original Swiss edition. With its American publication, it has assumed a definite American flavor. Adolf Guggenbühl-Craig has re-written the introduction providing a delightfully personal insight into his thinking. Sidney Handel's Commentary appears here for the first time in conjunction with Guggenbühl-Craig's writing and for the first time in English. Finally, the recasting of the language into the idiom of American readers is highlighted by the change of title.

   I would like to thank James Hillman for his invitation to do this book, Sidney Handel for his willing cooperation, and Mary Helen Gray Sullivan, the *eminence grise* of Spring Publications for her shepherding. Most of all I would like to thank Adolf Guggenbühl-Craig for shaking up the lethargy of my psyche.

Gary V. Hartman

Homo sum

Body and soul I hold in strictest rein,
But still does Satan cause me utmost pain.

&

I ever hate the city's arrogance
And gladly give a city child a chance.

&

I set great store by custom fine
And soon indulge accursed dice as mine.

&

Fist's tawdry law I hate withal
And have myself brought to a fall.

&

I pray like Christians for peace on earth,
And gorge myself on war and battle mirth.

&

So, I am no neatly finished box,
I am Man complete with paradox.

From *Hutten's Last Days*, XXVI
Conrad Ferdinand Meyer, 1871

INTRODUCTION

Perhaps because of the quality of paradox in my writings, I have frequently been asked what it is I actually believe in and why I seem to continuously pull back from directly stating my position. I have often posed the same question to myself. While I know that I have insights which fascinate and excite me at the time, these insights later appear questionable to me. Because everything appears questionable to such an extent, I easily succumb to the tendency to simply contradict general, collective opinions or to emphasize the other side. Even when a group is completely in agreement on some topic or other, I always tend to illuminate the so-called other side.

This little book best represents in some way or other how I truly see. I always see some thing and then, again, see its opposite. For me the world is an iridescent sphere, glittering with thousands of colors, colors which continually transform into other colors.

As a person, in personal relationships, I am not iridescent. It is enormously important for me to be loyal. I try to remain loyal to my friends, to my family, to my relatives and acquaintances, and to my country and my religion. There is nothing iridescent in that.

My form of opposition to collective opinion is, by the way, rather perverse and strange. The more I see the shadow side of something, the more I attempt to remain within it. I see, for example, the shadow side of psychotherapy and analysis quite clearly and have always tried to describe it just as clearly. I would never do what James Hillman has, namely to officially distance myself, at least temporarily, from psychoanalysis. I try to attack and, at the same time, to live in and have an effect upon what it is I am attacking. The more profoundly I come into contact with the shadow of psychotherapy, the more I persist in remaining loyal to the profession. The same principle applies to my place in society. I see the shadow side of Zürich social life quite distinctly and it upsets me tremendously again and again. On the other hand, I never even consider distancing myself from this society, rather I see myself very much as a part of it.

I have had this ambivalent attitude in every position I have ever filled. When I was president of the C. G. Jung Institute, I had to preside over examination conferences at times. During the first half hour I occasionally disapproved of, even hated my colleagues who were present. I had the impression that everything they said and did was truly ridiculous, if not downright immoral. In the course of the meeting my attitude would change somewhat and I could see that much of what was happening was interesting and important. By the time we concluded, my colleagues again appeared to be most interesting and decent people.

I realize I have not answered the question of what my real perspectives are, but I am not certain I can fully answer this question. Talking around my perspectives is, I believe, the best I can do.

In matters of religion I am an agnostic Christian. I take part in the Reformed Church, I have been a church warden, and I attend worship services regularly. I can not say, "Christ is really not the Son of God," or "He did not take away our sins by His death on the cross." Neither can I say that Christ has redeemed us and is the Son of God. I can only say that I am not really certain, but that I would like to remain a Christian and to continue to take seriously the basic assumptions of

Protestantism—the Apostles' Creed—and to continue to grapple with them. Not to take Christian Dogma seriously as a Christian seems unpsychological to me. At the same time I get upset at anyone who truly believes Christian Dogma.

It is obvious to me that all of us would also like the experience of God as mother, as feminine. I get perturbed, though, whenever feminists talk in these terms. I have the impression they believe that, by feminizing God, they comprehend Him and then they are completely off track.

I criticize Jungian Psychology roundly and Jung, himself, seems to me a most doubtful figure. In spite of that, I insist on calling myself a Jungian. I could never say I was an Archetypal Psychologist. I am and remain a Jungian, even though I have to at least question almost everything Jung wrote or said.

This little book is an attempt to grasp the ungraspable of the soul, to take the phenomenon of the soul seriously, completely seriously, and at the same time to make relative our knowledge of it. Dealing with soul is like dealing with God: We need to continuously grapple with it and to revere it. Yet how can we grapple with something and revere it when we are incapable of forming an image of it? My way of trying to form such an image is to continue to turn the sphere, allowing myself to be captivated by its iridescence and the way the colors change. I hope I have accomplished that in this book.

"Nothing is what it seems" has been one of the most important realizations that I have had in my life. The congenial businessman is brutally selfish at home; the moody, complaining family "dictator" has a heart of gold; the angelic, golden-curled child consistently behaves like a demon; the sunny inhabitants of the Mediterranean island cheat tourists up one side and down the other; and the glowering residents of a desert village are hospitality personified.

The saying, "appearances are deceptive," however, is not accurate in light of the following chapters. Appearances are just as "true" as what hides behind them. Jung supposedly said, "A psychological truth is only then true when the opposite is also true." We human beings are paradoxical beings and human psychology, therefore, is also paradoxical.

In this book I will address both individual humans and collective humanity through paradox and contradiction. At the beginning of each chapter, I have set a quotation which states a valid principle, a "truth." In the discussion which follows I will describe the exact opposite. Paradoxically, the quotation is just as much true as the content of the chapter it precedes.

CHAPTER 1

CREATIVITY, SPONTANEITY, INDEPENDENCE: THREE CHILDREN OF THE DEVIL

"The creative, spontaneous and independent human being is the goal of education." Anonymous, 1985

In a current psychological periodical, I came across this advertisement. "Course in Psychology — five weekends. How can you become creative, spontaneous and independent? Attending this course will enable you to develop your creativity, win back your spontaneity and become psychologically independent." The advertisement angered me. The words "creative," "spontaneous" and "independent" made my gall rise. I had often heard and read these three words in conjunction with psychology and apparently they touched a sore spot in me. I felt I had to get to the bottom of the matter for myself.

I become uncomfortable when people talk and write about a phenomenon so often and with such enthusiasm. The level of popularity leaves me with the impression that something is rotten in the state of Denmark. In the three concepts, creativity, spontaneity and independence, I imagined I sniffed something pathological. For this reason I will take a closer look at them in the following discussion.

Creativity

Let us first turn to creativity. What is creative? The majority of what we call "scientific" definitions of creativity are anything but creative. Here are several examples from psychology textbooks:

"Creativity can be defined quite simply as the ability to bring something new into being." This definition is a tautology: creativity is creativity.

"An idea is accepted as creative in the social system when it contains new or novel elements in a particular situation and when a meaningful contribution to problem resolution is seen." This is somewhat more complex, but does not take us very much further.

"Creativity is the ability to operate not merely from one perspective, but to consider and test out a variety of possibilities." This is certainly correct, but no deeper dimensions open up for us here.

Finally, I would like to quote Erich Fromm: *"Creativity means to become aware and to react or, the readiness to be born new each day."* Fromm's definition has the advantage that it uses an image, rebirth, but it is so general that it, too, is not much help for us.

Above all, I became uncomfortable with the mere term "creativity," believing therein to have smelled hidden psychopathology. In this regard, the above definitions were not much comfort. They failed to explain my unusual vexation. I will refrain from defining creativity, itself, since I have the impression that I am not creative enough to do so. I will say that we find creativity in the most widely differing activities of human beings; in art, in science, in technology, in psychology and so forth. There are apparently many kinds of creativity, but scarcely one satisfying definition.

Prior to the Renaissance, creativity as a concept, as an idea, as something of great import for the individual did not exist. Only in the sixteenth century did the notion of the "genius" in the sense of the creative man appear in Italy. Such a "genius" was understood to be an artist or engineer, someone who worked independently, who did not depend on the authority of antiquity. By the seventeenth century, the word genius had become an integral part of the Italian language in our present-day meaning of someone who is creative. English, French and German then adopted the word in the eighteenth century. "Genius" reached a high point in the nineteenth century when Cesare Lombroso, the famous Italian criminologist, wrote his well-known book, *The Man of Genius*. In this work, Lombroso portrayed genius as the essence of the creative man.

Today "genius" has lost something of its attraction; we speak of creativity instead. In our age it is almost a "must" to be creative. It is expected of us psychotherapists that we help our patients become creative. Everyone is supposed to develop his creativity, goes the thinking. The course I mentioned earlier is an example of how psychotherapists expect to help everyone become creative.

We should at least ask once and honestly, "Is everyone truly creative or at least potentially creative?" Certainly a great number of people are capable of very nice drawings and paintings. We encourage patients, for instance, to express themselves in so-called artistic ways. Their "creations" carry great significance for these patients and their therapists, represent spiritual life and promote psychic development. If, however, we were being unprejudiced, we would have to admit that such drawings, paintings and sculptures of patients are, as a rule, very collective and totally lacking originality. They contain no message for the general public, in no way do they have universal value and they offer nothing new.

Reversing positions, let us consider the psychological ideas of the majority of us psychologists and psychiatrists. By and large, our ideas are completely unoriginal and collective! We can hardly recognize any kind of creativity and even less something truly new in them. In form and content, these ideas are but repetitions or simply plain hard work. They are not genuinely creative, something very rare.

What about children's drawings? Children's paintings and drawings are touching, often even profound, moving the hearts of parents, surprising our friends and interesting therapists. When hung on the wall, however, usually they soon become boring. In my neighborhood, children spontaneously and on their own painted the walls of an underpass. They were likewise permitted to decorate some of the walls of their school. We were all enthusiastic and delighted, but after only six months these "works of art" had become increasingly tiresome until the adults wished that they would simply disappear.

We project so much onto children and onto what they produce. We project the divine child, an archetype which carries newness, freshness, hope and future. "Child" possesses qualities of being alive, not-yet-repressed and blossoming. In the primitivity and awkwardness of children's drawings, we believe we find our own lack of originality and freshness. As we withdraw these projections over time, what remains are only somewhat tiresome drawings, paintings or sculptures.

What really characterizes a truly creative human being? What is unique about an artist, for example, an innovative scientist, a ground-breaking psychologist or someone who otherwise is a genius in the sense of the Renaissance? How is such an individual different from the average citizen? The former's work, ideas, or insights have importance not only for himself or his family and friends, but are new and stimulating for a larger circle of humanity. This significance does not always manifest itself immediately and seldom goes uncontested, but is at least the goal of the activity.

Many creative individuals, artists especially, suffer from the delusion that they work only for themselves and in no way for the public at large. Yet, when this same public fails to value their work, artists often succumb to despair. When the artist does not experience it consciously, but represses the despair, it reappears in his dreams. "To show his work is vital for the artist, the *sine qua non* of his existence," wrote the French painter, Edouard Manet. To be appreciated by the public is an existential question for an artist. If a work of art never interests someone else, then perhaps it is because it is not art at all, but only the individual expression of the artist. Lacking any new message for general humanity, art may be purely personal. An artist wants to express more than the personal, to do more than depict only himself or heal more than himself.

The greatness of creative work appears to bear no real relationship to the individual personality and character of the creative human being. I have read many fascinating novels, seen various wonderful paintings, old as well as modern and marveled at numerous original ideas. When I subsequently have had the good fortune to personally meet and sometimes get to know the artist, author or scientist, I have usually been sorely disappointed. I have come to realize that the greatness of the work seems in no way to correlate with any kind of greatness of soul in the creator. I often, therefore, resolve not to spoil my pleasure or my admiration for the work, itself, by personal meetings with the originator.

Due to the play and the film, *Amadeus*, Mozart has recently received renewed popular attention. It is difficult for me to explain psychologically how this curious man could have created such divine music. Although his personality, life history and his being certainly influenced his music in many ways, his personality does not explain the godliness of his music.

Is this discrepancy between person and work really so astonishing? I believe it is only astonishing if we view creativity as something personal. I would like to postulate the following: the actual, meaningful character of a creative individual's work has little to do with that individual's personal psyche. To be sure, an author's mother complex, for example, will show itself in his novels. Life history, forefathers and family background all influence the themes and styles of poets and writers. Character and psychopathology find equal expression in the creations of novelists as well as patients. To the extent, however, that a creation touches others, touches the general public, it is much more than just the expression of a single person and his problems. It seems almost as though the genius, the creative individual, be he artist, author, or scientist, whoever creates in a non-personal way, is not, himself, creative.* "One must be able to say that this or that painting is the way it is in its power, because it is 'touched by God'," said Pablo Picasso.

Neither consciousness nor unconsciousness, neither the

creative individual nor the genius are themselves creatively active. *It* is creative, whatever this *it* may be, for creativity happens outside of the individual psyche. A highly gifted author of psychological books expressed it this way: "When I write, it seems to me that my fingers write on their own and not I, myself. My fingers play with the typewriter like autonomous beings." Phenomenologically, at least, it seems that a power external to the one creating is at work, that the creator is but a tool or vessel. How do I arrive at this hypothesis? First, my hypothesis is based on my experience with artists and creative individuals from a variety of fields, as I have already mentioned. My hypothesis also finds support in the word "gifted." "Gifted" means nothing less than that we possess something not part of ourselves, a gift, something that is given to us. The suprapersonal aspect of creativity finds further expression in the phrase "kissed by the Muses." Something other, the Muses, "gifts" or "kisses" the poet.

I believe that creativity is always impersonal, always transcends the personal. We should, therefore, speak of "transcendent creativity." The individual person is but an instrument having little or nothing to do with the creation. By the way, Freud says something similar. Freud emphasizes when speaking of the artist that he cannot say what determines an artist or what art is. He is only capable of writing about that which an artist expresses as a human being and how this shines through in a work of art. What art is, itself, Freud claims not to know.

I must immediately interject the following: Transcendent creativity is in no way a blessing for the vessel but more likely a curse. The message must be delivered, the work must be given form, even when the vessel or the tool breaks in the process. Such human beings *must* be creative, even when this means nothing other than to suffer. Yes, often the personality of the one in question is destroyed. The vessel is too small, the tool too weak. I am reminded of the tragic but highly popular example of Elvis Presley. He expressed something demonic/godly and he, himself, foundered on it. Alfred J. Ziegler, the noted Zürich psychiatrist and author, brought to my attention that in German the word *Kunst* (art) is as much related to *kuenden* (to announce) as to *koennen* (to be able). Perhaps we could say that the artist's ability lies in his capability to give voice, to announce, something beyond himself, something transcendent. That was certainly the power of Presley's voice! These are a few of my thoughts on the transcendent power of what we call creativity.

As I already mentioned, the concept of creativity carries another meaning and it would be remiss of me to simply leave this other usage by the wayside. I have mentioned the works of patients who express their purely personal problems in drawings, painting and the like. Not only do patients take delight in such activity, but many people sing, for instance and make music for the pleasure of their family and friends (or to their distress). Unendingly, much of what is termed "creativity" occurs everywhere human beings are found. Much of it is touching and it moves us in cases of people with whom we have some connection. The works themselves, though, have no further general significance.

I would like to designate all this activity, "personal creativity," in contrast to transcendent creativity. Personal creativity is abundant, can be found everywhere and is probably possible for everyone. All of us are, in the final analysis, something and have, therefore, something to express. We also speak of creativity in this personal sense; we apply the same word even though it is something completely different from transcendent creativity. Indeed, we should not refer to personal creativity as creativity at all. We might, for instance, speak of self-development, self-expression or something similar. In such cases, what we are referring to already exists and is neither something truly new nor something of wider significance. Despite the psychological importance of personal creativity, I dislike the fact that it tries to appropriate to itself the prestige and honor of transcendent creativity. Personal creativity has far less to do with suffering and with compulsion and produces nothing that goes beyond the purely personal.

We observe yet a third form of creativity which I would like to mention. We meet it often in those engaged in the fashion and advertising industry. Individuals with this variety of

---

*(Parenthetically, when I speak of the artist, author and so forth, I intend, as a matter of course, to include female artists and authors. Since I belong to the older generation, the masculine figures of speech carry, on one hand, the quality of maleness and, on the other, have universal significance, including both women and men.)

creativity are capable of conceiving designs which subsequently meet with great success in fashion sales. They possess, in other words, the ability to sense precisely what will come. It is not necessarily true that in fashion the great designers are the leaders in taste. Much more they possess an almost mediumistic gift of detecting what is playing itself out and forming in the soul of the collective. They recognize, for example, what kind of design and so forth will be in demand in the coming months and years.

Certainly there exist individuals among fashion designers with transcendent creativity. Often, however, they represent a form of creativity that I would like to designate "collective creativity." This form does not truly "create," but senses in advance what is taking place in the collective unconscious and makes use of it. From a negative perspective, we could characterize this type of creativity "hysterical." We find it frequently among writers or psychological authors, among individuals who foresee which ideas are on the ascendant and write about them. They have a nose for the collective trends and sniff out what the fashion will be.

We must, therefore, differentiate between transcendent creativity first, personal creativity second and collective creativity third. The term is the same with all three and yet represents three completely different things which, unfortunately, get confused constantly. Creativity enjoys a great deal of prestige, a prestige that properly belongs only to transcendent creativity. The other two forms are usurpers, so to speak, of the reputation of transcendent creativity. I can perhaps illuminate the standing of transcendent creativity with an image. By "transcendent" I mean, as I mentioned, something that comes through, shines through from another world. We could say that something of the Creator, something of God shines through. When we use this image, it is not out of place to assume that transcendent creativity brings us into connection with the divine and therefore justifies the high esteem it enjoys. The applause, the recognition for the creative does not belong — I wish to emphasize — to the vessel, but to the message the vessel conveys.

Many of us, though, have become "personal" to such an extent that we admire the vessel, the genius, the artist or the creative individual. We go so far as to assume the creative individual has something to tell us outside the area of his particular giftedness. Further, we believe that in order to understand his work, it is important to understand his personality. Art history, for instance, has tried repeatedly to connect the artist's personality with his art. In 1986, at the London School for Medical History, students were to write about the following topic: "Explain the relation between Freud's character and his psychological theories." In my opinion, the topic should have read the other way around, namely, "How did Freud's character deform the beauty, the originality of his psychological vision?" The question is not how Michelangelo's personality influenced his art, but how it interfered with it! The taste of the wine can be tainted by the container — wine in a plastic cup never tastes as good as wine in a glass. We can, however, never explain the taste of wine by the container alone.

We have gotten side-tracked a little here. Applying the same word, "creativity," to three completely different things, namely transcendent, personal and collective creativity, leads to a mix-up and a confusion of values. Transcendent creativity occurs rarely — most people do not possess a trace of it. As a rule, they are neither truly artistic, nor original, nor do they have any new ideas. We only copy, assimilate, adopt. We apply what other, original, creative individuals before us have made and created. As a rule, we are *creatures* and not *creators*. When I say, "we," I also mean we analysts. We view ourselves as having to use the ideas of others as precisely as possible since we are barely capable of developing any ourselves.

The confusion in the area of creativity is great. All of us long to transcend our mortal bounds. Since "transcendent" creativity offers the possibility of this experience, we revere it, look for it everywhere and demand it from everyone. Then we confuse messenger with message, seeing the former as more important than the latter. We search for something in the wrong place and end up worshipping idols. The result of this confusion is often detrimental to our psychological development.

Expecting everyone to be (transcendentally) creative is like expecting everyone to be an Old Testament prophet or the founder of a religion instead of simply followers of some established religion or religious form. Individuals who modestly move within one of the existing religious communities with no claim to originality succumb less to the great, sectarian movements of political and religious nature which always draw in countless others. Religion is a personal affair to be certain, but new religious forms and images are given to but a few.

Individuals who confuse their purely personal creativity — read, self-development, self-expression — with actual transcendent creativity, become addicted to an illusion and over-value themselves beyond measure. Generally, they are far from any religiosity but very near to a miserable self-cult. Analysis and psychotherapy understood wrongly can wreak great havoc here. Many upstanding, decent and simple people have discovered their so-called creativity in analysis — and begin to flood their environment, their room, their house — with the questionable products of their personal creation. They waste their time and have none left for reflection and, in particular, none for other relationships.

I am reminded of a woman who arranged marvelous social gatherings. The combination of the guests was, as a rule, stimulating and the culinary delights were outstanding. Through analysis she became "creative," expended a great deal of time giving expression to her soul in clumsy drawings and paintings and for years arranged no more gatherings.

Spontaneity

I will turn now to spontaneity. Our psychic life distinguishes itself by a changeable balance of different drives and archetypal forces which succeed in mutually balancing and holding each other in check or not. I am not completely certain whether all of our drives or archetypal forces always possess within themselves this checking action. With hunger, for example, this does not necessarily seem to be the case, otherwise there would not be so many individuals with eating disturbances.

We often complain about the lack of spontaneity and would like so much for love, especially, to express itself spontaneously more often. "*Ama fac quod vis*," — "love and you can do what you will." Unfortunately, love rules us but seldom. In the absence of *Eros* we are grateful for moral or other inhibitions and restrictions of our spontaneity. When love is not with us and such is often the case, then it is certainly useful for the dryness of morality to limit our spontaneity.

If we were truly spontaneous, we would give expression to all our negative impulses as well and often even resort to violence. Social life would hardly be possible under the rule of spontaneity. "I could just kill him," would then be more than a figure of speech. Furthermore, many men would sexually molest women continuously — and, naturally, the other way around as well. Infants crying in the night would be literally strangled should spontaneity truly rule. There would be no end to the horror. Of course, I am being simplistic with these possibilities. I wish only to note that, in spite of such scenarios, we consider complete spontaneity desirable.

Of the three children of the Devil, spontaneity is certainly the most appealing, the attribute we would least wish to be without. With no spontaneity, where would be the *beau geste*, where the innocent expression of tenderness and so forth. I will have more to say about spontaneity later.

To repeat what I said in the introduction, what the quotation at the beginning of this chapter says is just as true as my statements — this is the paradox of psychology. Psychological statements are especially valid when the opposite is also true. Someone else could sing the praises of these children — creativity, spontaneity and independence — just as easily as I characterize them as offspring of the Devil!

Independence

Let us turn now to independence, the third of our devilish trio. Psychological laymen and experts alike preach the importance of becoming independent — independent of mother, father, children, women, men, the collective, society and so forth. Is it not possible that our prized independence bears many similarities to a paranoid delusional system? What, exactly, is supposed to become independent — the ego? But the ego depends on the energy of the unconscious. And what is in this unconscious — the archetypes? Even the archetypes are not sole rulers, depending as they do on each other. Too, without the ego, archetypes could eventually get completely out of hand.

Should our destructiveness become independent, we could easily degenerate into muggers and murderers — think of the excesses of Nazi war criminals, Stalin's purges or the "cultural revolution" in China. Should the archetype of the dragon-slayer manifest its autonomy, we would alternate between the wildness of crusaders and cultic fanatics.

Since we are constantly connected with all of humanity through our collective unconscious, how can we possibly be "independent?" We all live in a complicated internal and external network of dependencies. Parents are continuously dependent on their children: the fate of their offspring influences fathers and mothers throughout their lives. Only parents devoid of feeling can say, "My daughter is now a thirty-year-old woman. What she does, what happens to her no longer concerns me. I am completely free of her — independent." Children depend on their parents even after their parents' death. Over and over I experience the post mortem coming to terms with parents, the *Auseinandersetzung*[1], not just as release, but also as the living out of fundamental connection. Neurotic seventy-year-olds are not the only people who call attention to themselves by how much they talk about their parents.

Marriage partners, too, not only love one another. They depend on each other in the depth of their beings (at least as long as the marriage lasts) and constantly influence each other, often even after divorce! While now and then material dependency increases with age, it usually decreases. By contrast, though, marriage partners are dependent their life long on the dynamics of the other's psyche.

As I mentioned, our psyche lives in a network of internal and external dependencies. Instead of struggling against our dependencies, would it not be wiser to reflect on them and to attempt to locate and develop our soul *within* them? We would further our psychological development more by realizing that psychic life *is* dependence and that, therefore, we would do well to shape and form our dependence.

Not all eras and cultures have been so enthusiastic about independence. A Japanese psychiatrist explained to me that *amai*, the Japanese word for human connection, can best be translated as "loving dependence." This emphasis on dependence in relationship has specific consequences. We in the West would say to a guest, "If you are hungry, just go to the refrigerator and help yourself." We would like to encourage him to feel at home in our kitchen. Apparently, this way of doing things would be confusing if not insulting to a guest in Japan. There the guest is honored when his host hands him a dish of vanilla ice cream with the request to, "Please eat." A guest would never serve or help himself, rather he is dependent in his choices. While in Europe it might be more polite to ask, "Would you care for tea or coffee," in Japan one would say, "You would certainly like a cup of coffee." A host decides for his guest and the latter recognizes the freedom of this dependency. In the West, couples in love are among the few to happily admit their mutual and complete dependency on their beloved with statements such as, "I can't live without you," and the like.

God Complex

To recapitulate, I have tried to show that various forms of creativity exist, among which only one deserves to be called, "creative," namely "transcendent" creativity. To "possess" this form of creativity is as difficult for its bearer as its occurrence is rare. The other forms of creativity, personal and collective, profit from the prestige which transcendent creativity enjoys. When, however, we confuse the other forms with true creativity, we experience a damaging delusion of grandeur as the result.

I have further established that spontaneity and independence are of but doubtful psychological value. At the same time we cannot simply devalue something that currently is so esteemed. If thousands of psychotherapists, judges, ministers, teachers, professors, philosophers and so forth assert that modern man should be creative, spontaneous and independent, then we must be able to find something desirable in these three psychological phenomena. Let us examine our trinity from a mythological and archetypal standpoint. Can we not discern some kind of myth concealed here? Could we even discover behind this triad an archetypal psychopathology?

The word "creativity" comes from the Latin *creare*, "to create." We name God our "Maker," the "Creator," and human beings we name "creatures." To be creative is an attribute of God's: God created heaven and earth, created us and all living beings. He is, therefore, creative — yes, *only* God is truly creative. Based on this perception, Protestant circles of the 19th Century rejected the usage of the word creative in conjunction with human activities. They viewed the usage as sinful, prideful and arrogant.

I want to mention something else concerning the "anti-creative" tradition. In the oldest synagogues of the Middle East there was often a *cathedra*, a chair, which stood in readiness for Moses and upon which no one ever sat. Moses was very close to God and through Moses, God created the Jewish Law. No one besides Moses was able to be creative, a tradition which found the following expression. Until the late 19th Century, orthodox rabbis went to the greatest lengths never to be original. If any of them had an original idea, he had to conceal it behind endless citations from the Talmud. In no way might he give the impression that he felt himself in the least to be original or creative. We are dealing, therefore, with two traditions. On the one hand, creativity is admired. On the other, it is regarded as an exclusive attribute of God and any human claims to it can only be seen as *hubris.*

Even so, creativity brings us face to face with God. Can we say the same thing for independence? We can certainly assume that the only truly independent being in the world is God. By definition, God is independent from everything and everything is dependent on Him. He is beginning and end, *Alpha* and *Omega* of creation. Whether Christian, Jewish or Islamic, God is totally independent. In addition, only God can be completely spontaneous with no fear of punishment. His spontaneity is most troublesome for us: God does not have to justify Himself to anyone. His moods, though, influence the course of the world. In his anger He sent the Flood. After the

Flood, regretting what He had done, He promised never again to destroy humanity. Should He ever again become angry, however, nothing can stop His sweeping mankind away with, for example an atomic catastrophe. We cannot reason with God.

As you know, C. G. Jung suggested another conception of God, a God who is also dependent upon us, that is, not totally independent nor completely spontaneous. Jung's notion of God has not prevailed — perhaps, not yet? We struggle today with the Christian, Islamic, Judaic concept, the concept of a God creative, spontaneous and totally independent. Seen from the perspective of the collective religious currents, the Christian God has in recent times lost significance and influence, at least in Europe. In the 19th Century, for instance, every passenger on an Atlantic crossing prayed regularly every morning. This sort of religiosity is hardly imaginable today. Do we moderns not simply put ourselves in the place of God? Do we not believe that we are like God? Instead of worshipping the creative, independent and spontaneous God, we seem to view ourselves as creative, independent and spontaneous, at least potentially. Here we are on the trail of a pathology, the trail of a God complex or of an identification with God.

I must elaborate on something at this point. It is to Jung's credit historically that he clearly differentiated between ego and Self. Unfortunately, many psychological authors in adopting the concept of the Self, albeit without crediting Jung, have caused confusion. The ego deals with the ordering of the interior world and with coordinating our relationship to the environment. The Self is the center of the psyche, the vehicle by which we experience meaning. We could say it is the divine spark in us, that which brings us into relationship with God in our psyches. Some psychologists are of the opinion that God is nothing other than a projection of the Self outside ourselves. I am not so certain. God is significantly more than a projection of some psychic force or energy. What we do project is our longing for oneness with God.

We partially project the desire for oneness backwards, regressively, as represented by the myth of the paradise in which Adam and Eve lived and from which they were expelled. We

¹"Grappling with," " coming to terms with."

often misread the myth, however. We assume it refers to a kind of memory of our earliest childhood when the world was still undivided. I believe the notion that in earliest childhood we were one with our mother and through her with the world, what Margaret Mahler calls "symbiosis," is as much a myth as the one of paradise. The Garden of Eden is a religious myth; the idea of infant oneness is the corresponding psychological myth.

I suspect that life is extremely difficult for us all from the very beginning. Hardships begin in our mother's womb. In the fetal stage we are exposed to all kinds of hormonal and emotional storms through our mother, storms which we do not understand and which we can do nothing about. As soon as we catch sight of the light of the world, we are further exposed to cold, heat, hunger and other unpleasant sensations. Not only can we not grasp these sensations, but we have to deal with the ambivalent feelings from human beings around us including our mother. Paradise in childhood, oneness with mother, as I have said, is nothing but the concretized, misunderstood mythology of paradise.

We also project our longing for oneness with God into the future, onto the kingdom to come, the heavenly mansion of many rooms. At the end of days, evil and suffering will be conquered and death will have lost its sting. This future projection promises complete bliss. Our yearning for utopia is another form of the projection of oneness into the future, one which Communist leaders, among others, have made use of. Their message is: "Things are bad now, but soon we will have paradise on earth."

The two mythologies, paradise lost and the kingdom to come, express exactly what they describe. We mortal beings are never truly united with God. We long for union and either believe we have experienced it in the past or hope we will find it in the future. Perhaps, there actually *was* a reality of union when the world began, and perhaps we will experience it in our present incarnated existence. What we do experience is nothing less than a state of being cut off from God. Much human, existential suffering comes from this separation, just as much longing comes from the hope of release from the separation.

This suffering and this longing can lead to an archetypal kind of pathology. We attempt to resolve the separation from God by becoming like God; we wish to *be* God. At the same time we realize the discrepancy. We realize that we are not God, that the Tower of Babel was not completed and that Heaven has not been taken by storm. In many stories the Devil promises to fulfill all of our wishes when we pay his price. The Devil, though, is a part of God, the shadow of God. So in reality, God's shadow awakens in us the wish to be like God. (I get into difficulties here mythologically and start to become confused.) When educators, ministers and therapists of all kinds, all of us, encourage creativity, spontaneity and independence, all attributes of God, they are taking the Devil's side. They are encouraging us to become God, speaking imaginatively. They appeal to the God complex, working in conjunction, to stay with the image, with Satan, with God's shadow. Patients should, therefore, give special attention to a therapist's shoes: there may be a cloven hoof in them!

Before I continue on the subject of the God complex, I want to do something odd, something that corresponds to the mythology of the Devil but not completely with the logic of my argument. I want to play *advocatus diaboli* for a moment. The God complex is so wonderful and fascinating that we are loath to do without it. It gives us a powerful feeling of being uplifted, of being important, at least for a time.

I once knew a flute teacher who, for years, gave lessons to students with varying degrees of talent. She suffered from sleep disturbance and finally went into analysis. Her analyst encouraged her, or her dreams encouraged her, to give concerts. She was completely untalented as a soloist, but her concertizing made her unbelievably happy. After the performances she felt like she was walking on air and she looked radiant. Her sleep disturbance disappeared for a while. Even her audiences, consisting mostly of friends and relatives, were deeply impressed, not by the music, but by the fact that the concerts appeared to completely transform the woman. Without this passing phase of inflation, the woman would perhaps have remained stuck in her sleep disturbance; the Devil had at least gotten things moving. Of course, there was also a price to pay. The woman began to direct her aggression toward her family and her ability to reflect diminished. She became extremely tiresome for those around her. I mention this story as an aside and will now return to the God complex and its further discussion.

During the 18th and 19th Centuries, the educated public greatly occupied itself with so-called insane asylums. Laymen had a very definite conception of the inmates of these public institutions. They imagined that one patient believed himself to be Napoleon, another to be Caesar or Alexander the Great and yet another the King of Kings or Emperor of the Universe or even God, Himself. All of these figures, Napoleon, Caesar, Alexander and so forth, are men who suffered from a God complex, who identified with God or a god either openly or in secret, who believed themselves a divine incarnation.

I find it psychologically meaningful that these psychotics so occupied the interest of people living in the last two centuries. Their interest progressed to the point that they believed the majority of inmates suffered from delusions of grandeur and identification with God. The actual number of psychotics with this diagnosis was not so large. People apparently assumed the essence of psychosis, the core of madness, to be the belief that one was God or at least similar to God. The height of madness found its utterance in the God complex, a fundamental psychopathology.

Consciously or unconsciously, all human beings wish to come closer to God. This is an archetypal truth. Wishing to be God or believing I *am* God is probably an archetypal psychopathology. As I have shown, the notion that creativity, independence and spontaneity should be the goal of psychological development is tied to the God complex. But perhaps I am being too gentle. The collective idea that everyone should be or become creative, independent and spontaneous as much as possible is a mental disorder. Such a goal is *hubris* and *hubris* for the ancient Greeks who coined the term, was extremely dangerous. It led to random acts of violence due to the identification with the deity and was always punished severely.

We need to ask why the God complex—through the reverence for our unholy trinity—plays such an important role today. That psychotherapists of all kinds promote this reverence is not particularly unusual. We are to some extent but priests of the collective spirit, preaching and mediating general thinking and collective psychopathology. Let me pose the question again: Why does the God complex have so much collective significance at this moment in time? I must assume that it has always been significant given the kings, emperors, pharaohs and rajas who insisted on their divinity (Louis XIV of France, the *roi soleil*, comes to mind). With the spread of democracy, the God complex, too, experienced a "democratization." The God complex currently hides behind the idea that every individual should or could be creative, spontaneous and independent.

Self-Effacing Therapy

All this compels me to plead the cause of Self-Effacing Therapy, of self-effacing analysis and self-effacing psychology. I am opposed to any therapy and any psychology that has succumbed to or lapsed into the God complex. Since neither we therapists nor our clients are geniuses, the "effacing" part of this approach should not be terribly difficult. In fact, so few of us on either side fall into the genius category that it is not worth mentioning from a psychotherapeutic perspective. I offer an example of someone who was pushed into a creative role, of someone who, in short, did not undergo self-effacing therapy.

The analysand I have in mind was a thirty-year old, somewhat depressive man. His mother had always told him he was a genius and his wife had carried on this mythology. In his analysis he freed himself from his mother's fantasy but his analyst assumed the fantasy, thereby thrusting the unfortunate into "creativity." Since he possessed a certain writing ability— he wrote his dreams quite well—he began to devote himself to general writing and contented himself for years in passing his time with worthless scribbling. In so doing, the real joys and sorrows of his life passed him by.

Self-effacing therapy would free us, would make us happy and content not to be creative, to be free from transcendent creativity. It would make us content to value what most of us are, namely, not creative. It would help us to thankfully appreciate the fruit of the work of genuinely creative individuals without, ourselves, having to suffer from our talent or perishing from it. What I call personal creativity can develop successfully without false aspirations. Self-effacing therapy recognizes, for example, that only one in a billion will be the founder of a new religion. None of us, therefore, should succumb to pressure to find our completely personal religion, but rather to modestly align ourselves with one of the established religions.

Furthermore, self-effacing therapy means taking on dependence. It means realizing that we are only small cogs in a giant mechanism, that everything and everyone depend upon everything and everyone — father, mother, children, husband, wife, friends, society, culture and so forth. We *can* live out this dependence in happiness and contentment. How much does our continual pushing and shoving toward God-like independence block valuable psychological development? Psyche shows itself in dependence. I do not, therefore, consider it necessarily good when a patient's medical history states, "The patient succeeded in freeing himself from his dependence upon his mother. Currently, he only sees his mother about four times a year, whereas earlier he talked to her on the telephone every week and visited her twice a month." I think it would be better if the chart stated instead, "The patient is very much bound to his mother by innumerable ties that go back and forth between him and her. The patient is aware of the many contradictory feelings in this relationship. He hates and loves his mother in a much more differentiated way."

Finally, self-effacing therapy could result in our mistrusting spontaneity somewhat more than we do.

Self-effacing therapy would mean that as clients, patients and analysands — and as therapists — we recognize how non-creative, how lacking in spontaneity and how dependent we are. We would recognize that it is not necessary to take these expectations upon ourselves and thus be driven into a desperate inflation. Self-effacing therapy invites us to live as most of us truly are and not to have to measure ourselves with the yardstick of individuals who are cursed with a talent or a gift. Individuals with genius are transcendentally creative and to that degree independent and spontaneous. They are only vessels, only tools for the creative, spontaneous and independent message. They pay and suffer fearfully for the message, a problem particular only to them. For the rest of us, the problem is to suffer the way we are and not to demand of ourselves that we be unique vessels, creative and equal to God.

Self-effacing therapy helps us to accept our condition as it is and, naturally, to value and take pleasure from genius where it appears. It helps us also to be glad that we are hardly ever vessels of otherworldly messages and therefore suffer less. We should be thankful for our lack of creativity, spontaneity and independence and, at the same time, appreciate the fascinating offerings of creative individuals. Here is an example of what I am talking about. I knew a man of about fifty years of age who had a certain amount of acting ability. Never did he consider becoming an actor, himself. In his free time, however, he worked as a volunteer stage hand for a small theater group where his presence always encouraged the actors. He recognized that he was not blessed and cursed with talent. At the same time, he could participate in and enjoy the theater in a way that was satisfying to him. This is what I mean about humbly being what we are.

Insofar as we clients, patients or therapists content ourselves to live with our human nature and not to deviate into the God complex or the Self complex — and here is the paradox — we probably come closer to the Self and the divine spark in ourselves. Insofar as we recognize our human limitations, we certainly come much closer to God than when we succumb to the God complex in its triune expression of creativity, spontaneity and independence.

Nothing that I have said in the foregoing pages is in any way new nor is it at all creative. Perhaps in this chapter I have strayed too far into the no-man's-land between religion and psychology — something of course that is difficult to avoid in psychology. In the next chapter, I will attempt to keep my discussion more purely psychological.

CHAPTER 2

SINISTER FATHERS—HEALTHY CHILDREN

"He will, himself, be that much more loving a father, The more loving a father he has to remember." Johann Jakob Engel, 1745-1777 *"German Philosopher for the World"*

Parents do much harm, a chain of harm that winds its way throughout the history of humanity. Parental failure, poor child rearing, is the cause of much personal misfortune, of much unsuccessful psychological development. Let me put it a bit differently. Had our parents not themselves been harmed by *their* parents, there would be far fewer neurotic and psychotic people in this world. Had they not been harmed, our parents would not have harmed us, their own children. We are not born bad, harmful parents; it is not integral to human nature to be a bad father or a bad mother. In psychological literature, though, we often encounter the image of harmful parents who, by their nature, damage innocent, healthy children—an image which today influences professionals and nonprofessionals alike. For the purposes of this chapter, I am going to put mother aside and direct my attention to father, the stepchild of modern developmental psychology.

A child's healthy development, according to current psychological thinking, requires not only a somewhat loving mother, but also a somewhat loving father. Classical mythology presents us with a different perspective in countless tales of harmful, even murderous, fathers. Chronos swallowed his children, Demeter, Hades, Hera and Zeus, when they were born out of fear they might endanger his position as ruler. Chronos' father, Uranos, threw his children into the depths of Hades into Tartarus. Tantalus served to the gods his son, Pelops, as a meal. Even the revered Biblical father, Abraham, was prepared to kill his son, Isaac, because he believed God had ordered him to do so. Mythologically, the murderous father is just as important and significant as the kindly, loving father.

Freudian mythology also knows an extremely destructive father. In *Totem* and *Taboo*, Freud describes the image of the primal horde. While the old father ruled at home, the sons were forced to disappear into the jungle without taking wives for themselves. Finally, the sons banded together, killed the old man, and ate his body—certainly a striking mythological image. (Although Freud is without a doubt the most significant mytho-poet of modern time, only Jungians can truly grasp the beauty of his mythology.)

If it is true that mythological stories symbolically represent archetypes, then "father" certainly has many sinister, even murderous, aspects. Such aspects are not only the result of early childhood trauma, but are in the nature of father. The destructive, murderous father is perhaps as fundamental as the kind, loving father. We may find this reality somewhat disorienting. In the following lines I offer an illustration of what I mean.

A thirty-year-old business woman, married and mother of two children, began psychotherapy because she suffered from periodic, stubborn sleeplessness. She had been an only child, growing up in what outwardly appeared to be a stable family. Her mother was loving and kind. Her father, in contrast, was a talented ne'er-do-well and family tyrant who tended toward alcoholism. Both mother and daughter often lived in fear of him. At 16, the patient left the family, completed a business apprenticeship and finally founded a business which she ran very successfully with her partner. She often dreamed about her father, but during months of analysis, she did not mention her father's destructive and sinister sides. When, during a session, she did talk about her terrible experiences with her father, it made a profound impression on me and I felt great sympathy for her. The woman could not accept my sympathy and said, "You misunderstand me. Of course, I missed having a good, loving father. The continual fear of his outbursts of rage made me almost physically ill as a child. In spite of that, my father gave me a great deal through just that destructive side. Without that experience I would not be who I now am. I can only pity women who only knew a kind and loving father."

In the following months we worked intensively with her relationship with her father. I realized she truly did not reject her father unequivocally. She was even thankful to him for having shown her a genuine side of fathering, namely, the destructive one. She truly *did* pity children who only experienced a loving father. This patient confused me. How was I supposed to understand her? Should not her father have been a terrible problem for her? Should she not have suffered from an extremely negative father complex?

"Father" is archetypal and, like any archetype, has two sides. On the one hand, father protects, educates, guides, loves and cares. On the other, he rages, destroys, murders and castrates. The actual father reflects all these characteristics, living them out and incarnating them. Just like the archetype, the actual father's feelings toward his children are partially loving, tender and caring, but also partially destructive, almost murderous. The latter feelings can be evoked, for example, when an infant cries all night long or when a teenager begins to rebel. As a rule, the father is ashamed of his negative emotions. His outbursts of archaic, negative feelings astonish him. He may even realize the important role these same feelings play in cases of child abuse. In my experience, fathers who mistreat their children are not always psychotic, malicious sadists, incapable of loving and showing tenderness. Mostly, they are clumsy in expressing their feelings and are in no way a match for the archaic power of their emotions. Faced with these demonic emotions, the fathers' mistreatment of their children is but the manifestation of the difficulty they experience with the products of their own psyches.

Although the destructive, murderous father is as archetypal as the loving one, the image of the kindly father exerts a powerful influence on all fathers as a collective expectation. Modern psychology views a father's destructive feelings as condemnable, a sign of immaturity, of infantility or as the result of early childhood trauma. For the development of the human soul, particularly for individuation, confronting the archetypes completely is of crucial significance. We need to experience the archetypes in all their dimensions in our fellow human beings as well as through our inner images and emotions. In meeting our concrete fathers we also come to terms, at least partially, with the father archetype.

Many children are fortunate enough to experience a father who lives and expresses the sinister *and* the loving side of the archetype. Yet many also experience a father in whom these polarities are not balanced, one being stronger than the other for whatever reason. To experience a father who incarnates only one extreme, be it the loving or the destructive one, a father in whom one of the opposites remains hidden, is a great loss for a child's development. The worst possibility is to experience no father at all or one who can live neither the destructive nor the loving aspect of the archetype. Strangely enough, in my experience it does not seem to matter so much whether a child experiences the destructive or the caring side. Of greatest importance is that he or she experiences at least *one* side of the father archetype in his or her concrete father — or at least in a father figure.

The image, the mythologem, of the one-sidedly or primarily positive father, tyrannizes actual fathers, forcing them to deceive both themselves and the outer world. While they constantly simulate the "good father," they feel guilty whenever they encounter the destructive side in themselves. Consequently, fathers do not confront the negative aspect of the archetype at all and its destructive energy withdraws into the deepest layers of the psyche, into the unconscious.

Let me repeat what I have just said. While all archetypes work and live continuously in us, we have the option of confronting them to a greater or lesser degree. If we fail to relate to parts or even entire archetypes in our surroundings, they assume archaic, demonic form. It is almost impossible to come to terms with archetypes at such a level, in which case we have to constantly project them outward onto someone or something that resembles the repressed, unlived psychic content.

In the course of my life, I have met many young people who experienced only the loving father in the outer world. They were, therefore, never forced to grapple with the murderous side of the archetype in their environment or in themselves. These young people subsequently projected the destructive portion of the father archetype onto the world around them, using the smallest of hooks on which to hang their projections. Every mildly authoritarian or domineering male figure became a murderous, inhuman father. Because they had not learned to deal with the destructive side of father, they became existentially insecure when they met anything that even resembled it. I have heard young people from solid, middle-class families yell out, "Cops are pigs, murderers, not humans!" Policemen were no longer human beings in their eyes. They were living representations of the destructive side of the father archetype with which the young people could not come to terms.

The patient I mentioned earlier was in contact with the archetype's destructive part from her earliest youth. She knew him as an outside and an inside figure. She developed the capability of dealing with her fear whether she met with him in the outside world or in herself. According to current psychological wisdom, she should have continuously projected the destructive father onto the outer world. That is precisely what she did not do. She was conscious of and familiar with the sinister, threatening qualities of the father archetype, brought closer to her through the behavior of her biological father.

At this point, the reader will now certainly protest and exclaim, "Does it really not matter in the least for the development of children whether their fathers manifest primarily the destructive or the protective aspect of the father archetype? Would it not be best for children to experience the kindly and protective father, less desirable for them to encounter the loving *and* the destructive father, and least desirable for them to experience no father at all? Finally, would not the worst of all possibilities be for them to have to come to terms with only the destructive energy of fathering?" I do not think so. I would rank the possibilities as follows: Best would be to encounter the negative *and* the positive sides; second best would be to experience only the positive or only the negative; and worst would be to not experience father at all. At the same time, we might remember the admonition of the satirist, Wilhelm Busch: "First it happens differently and second than one thinks." I will return to these questions later.

I ask myself whether it is desirable to attempt to only play "good father?" Would it not perhaps be better, as I suggested above, to be genuine and truthful to some extent, to manifest and live both aspects of the father, the positive and the negative? Repressing the negative father brings a variety of consequences, only one of which is the abuse of children.

Child abuse of all kinds occupies the focus of public attention today and rightly so. We must do everything in our power to protect children from violence. Whenever something is so central in the general interest, however, there is some correlation with the facts. Child abuse, for instance, *is* widespread and deplorable. At the same time, general interest is also an expression of the psychological situation of the collective and the individuals interested in the phenomenon. I suspect the more the mythological image of the primarily good father predominates in society, the more the image of the destructive father will appear as an expression of the repressed polarity of father as archetype. We might view the fascination with child abuse as the opposite extreme of the dominant mythology of the loving father. I will speak of this theme, sexual misuse of children, in another context in a later chapter.

When the image of the good father rules collectively, that of the destructive father makes its appearance. The destructive aspect will then (and rightly so) be seen more clearly or have a greater fascination. We must recognize that not only objective facts and situations stimulate our interest, but our psychological condition, our one-sidedness, does as well. Whenever any phenomenon becomes the focal point of public attention, therefore, we have to ask ourselves, "How is it that we are suddenly so occupied with this or that subject? To what end does it upset and confuse us so much?" We could pose further questions. "Why is it that the image of the good father—or the good mother—is so prevalent? Why does the collective regard the positive side of the image as the sole or correct one? What perspective or which mythology—consciously or unconsciously—forms the backdrop for these contemporary attitudes?"

The spirit of precision from the natural sciences still rules our current thinking. Natural science, though, sails under the flag of causality, at least in its practical application. Only theoretical physics sees the world differently, no longer assuming the predictability of the behavior of individual molecules, of the simple chain of cause and effect. Fundamentally, however, causality rules the natural sciences and our human collective. We psychologists, as a part of the collective, continually attempt to find causes, to discover what the causes for the healthy or pathological development of human beings might be.

In the 19th Century, many physicians believed that masturbation was the determining cause of unfavorable psychological development. Today we identify the parents as the primary root of all kinds of psychopathology. Parents are responsible for lack of mirroring, Oedipal complexes and sexual expressions between parents and children (once viewed concretely, later seen symbolically and, again today, understood concretely). Many researchers assume that the majority of severely neurotic or psychotic adults were sexually abused as children. Sometimes working mothers are regarded as the cause of all misery. Then again, psychologists see the cause in mothers who choose to stay home, but later, regretting their decision not to pursue careers, become angry and frustrated with their children. Scapegoats are many and varied: castrating, tyrannical fathers; weak fathers; absent fathers; the matriarchy ("Mommism"); the patriarchy; repression of women; repression of the feminine; lack of sexual education; or premature sex education.

We psychotherapists search continually for psychological sources of mental disorders. We do so not only because the model of causality rules our thinking, but because each new-found cause provides us anew with the hope of being better able to heal. If, we believe, we only knew the origin of the disturbance, we would have the possibility of healing or at least of prevention.

We might ask ourselves which mythology hides behind the natural sciences with its belief in cause and effect? Perhaps the myth is the one of dominion over nature. It could be the myth of Prometheus who stole fire — energy — from the gods, or the myth of the tower of Babel — storming the heavens. It could be the myth of the serpent in paradise who told Adam and Eve, "You will become like God," or the myth of space travel from comic strips and films where different forces vie for control of the universe. Interestingly enough, the last few years have seen the appearance of a line of children's toys called, "Masters of the Universe." While these mythologies of cause and effect perhaps suffice for our relationship with nature, their limitations are only gradually becoming more obvious. Given our capacity to manipulate nature based on cause and effect, in time we will not only control nature but possibly also destroy it.

Even so, the law of cause and effect simply does not apply to matters of the soul or psyche. Cause and effect do not regulate the soul. Understood scientifically, causality means that the same cause always results in the same effect. Cause and effect rule the fields of physiology and physical medicine, for instance. We understand — and perhaps heal — a physical disease if we are able to describe its symptoms, know its prognosis and identify its causes.

Jungian psychology assumes that the endless search for causes and the belief in our capacity to heal once we have identified these causes are nothing but a dead end. Admittedly, a variety of factors affect the psyche: inheritance, physical and chemical structure of the brain, the lymphatic system, the body in general, the environment, parents, social milieu and so on. Therapy for psychological disorders must take all of these considerations into account, but not exclusively.

An old conflict in psychology is whether inheritance or environment determines us as human beings, the question of "nature or nurture?" Certain psychologists and philosophers advanced the notion that environment, including education and social milieu, represents the determining factor. Others, again, rejected this theory. They assumed that inherited structures form the basis for all of our behavior. Still others maintained that both environment and inheritance determine human nature. All three positions, however, ignore the soul.

Jung insisted repeatedly on the *autonomy of the soul*. In other words, the soul is not "caused," neither by nature, inheritance, nor by the environment and education. The soul is independent, autonomous and can not — or only conditionally — be understood via the category of cause and effect. Therefore, we cannot predict human behavior, neither that of individuals nor that of groups and societies. Who could have foreseen three years ago that East Germany, the best organized Communist state, would have collapsed in the immediate future? Who could have foretold that the brutal soldiers of the German Democratic Republic would have become fundamental protectors of freedom and democracy? Such is indeed the case. Within a matter of months those horrific instruments of tyranny have been integrated into the army of West Germany, a member nation of NATO!

In spite of multiple theoretical considerations to the contrary, the man on the street recognizes that the soul is autonomous, that it does not follow the law of cause and effect. We never, for example, experience our decisions as having been caused. We firmly believe that we, ourselves, arrive at decisions with the full potential to decide one way or the other. Should we determine to go to the movies some evening, we do not think of this decision simply as the outcome of set factors that leave us no other choice. By and large, we experience our conclusions as free decisions not dependent upon cause and effect.

Let us now take up the theme of father once more. Although Jung continually emphasized the autonomy of psychic functioning, the fact is that the mythology of causality dictates our thinking as Jungians to some extent. We must, so we believe, find causes in order to be able to heal. Even for many Jungians, parents become the cause of pathology in children. The destructive, uncaring father and the destructive, uncaring mother are cases in point.

Besides causality, a further mythologem exerts considerable influence in this thought pattern we are exploring: Good leads to Good; Evil leads to Evil. Voltaire, for one, wrote, "Good never produces Evil." This bizarre perspective, this peculiar mythological understanding, strongly affects our unconscious even though literature and mythology in general have very different stories to tell.

Mephistopheles tells Faust, "I am the force that always wills Evil and always creates Good." In addition, we can turn to the classical story of Oedipus. Desiring to be a good and upstanding individual, he became the victim of tragic mistakes as a result. He learned through the oracle that he would kill his father and marry his mother. To avoid such disgrace, he left his foster parents whom he believed to be his parents, met and killed his actual father and married his actual mother!

Nowhere is the psychological reality of mankind demonstrated so clearly as in literature. The consequences of evil, aggressiveness and destructiveness are sometimes positive and often negative. Love and friendship can produce helpful but often deleterious effects. Evil can lead to Evil *and* to Good, and the other way around. Nowhere is there conformity. Even the Marquis de Sade was wrong when he asserted that virtue leads always to degeneration and vice to happiness.

What is the significance of the above considerations for our topic of the moment? They signify that the children of good, or of more or less good, parents are often healthy *and* often extremely neurotic. Further, they signify that children of bad parents, or relatively bad parents, are often neurotic *and* often extremely strong, healthy, and happy. Anything is possible! We might well ask, therefore, where this naive image comes from that Evil leads to Evil and Good to Good? Why is the image so incredibly powerful?

I suspect that the image has to do with our Christian

heritage, that it represents a degeneration and perversion of Christian mythology. Jesus is victorious over Satan, at least at the Last Judgment. Sinners go to hell. The righteous go to heaven. Jesus, the Good, wins. Satan, the Evil, loses forever. The victory of Gentle Jesus — "gentle" being a caricature of the figure of Jesus — remains a dominant Christian image even today. Concretized, the earthly variation of this mythological image is that Good triumphs and that Evil loses. Evil causes Evil and so forth. Expressed paradoxically, I could say that this Good/Good, Evil/Evil image is extremely damaging in human psychology. It is even more damaging when it is combined with the belief in causality!

One-Sided Mythological Images

While we talk a great deal about mythology, we are usually not critical enough of the images it provides us. Mythological images can, for example, be very one-sided and, for this reason, harmful. The one-sidedness of the image of the predominantly good father can have as damaging an effect as that of causality. There are numerous one-sided mythologems and images: the noble hero who slays the dragon comes to mind. We know countless such dragon slayers: St. George, the patron saint of England and of soldiers; St. Michael, the patron saint of policemen; Apollo, who killed the dragon that sleeps in the earth at Delphi.

As we might expect, there of course exist various mythological possibilities for coming to terms with the dragon. One legend claims that St. George did not kill the dragon but only tamed it. We are also familiar with tales of dragons who hold maidens captive. The hero appears, kills the monster, and carries the maiden home. This latter variation of the dragon stories is somewhat less one-sided since it suggests transformation. The dragon and the virtuous maiden are, perhaps, one and the same. The one whom the hero carries home and marries shows her dragon side later through becoming a shrew. (In German we call someone who is a shrew a "house dragon.")

As Jungians we usually assume that the hero who kills

the dragon represents a symbol of the ego. By conquering the motherliness of being unconscious, the ego frees itself. Such all-too-simplistic understanding of the dragon fight is but another expression of the dragon-slayer motif. Inasmuch as the fearful, demonic dragon—understood as the motherly unconscious—is slain, we fall victim to a pseudo-clarity. We convince ourselves that darkness is overcome and clarity rules. We understand all kinds of psychological phenomena lying clearly before us in the light of our consciousness. We live out this misleading, dragon-slayer myth when we believe we completely understand our patients' dreams. It is worse still, when we think that we completely comprehend our patients—or any of our fellow human beings—to any ultimate degree.

I have occasion to read lots of case reports written as part of their training by candidates of the C. G. Jung Institute in Zürich. Some of them are quite outstanding. Others, however, are extremely irritating. Candidates frequently attempt—with apparent success—to explain everything—every personality trait, every suffering and pleasure, each pathology—that the case in question presents. Everything is "perfectly clear." Case X, for example, has to do with the result of early childhood wounding or with sexual abuse as a child or with a lack of mirroring. C. G. Jung polemicized frequently against our tendency to reduce everything complicated to something simple, as Freud did in reducing the totality of psyche to sexuality. The tendency toward reductionism is a radical form of dragon slaying. All that is difficult, dark or chaotic has to be traced back to what seems precise and exact.

The image of the dragon slayer, of the shining hero, of the ego that is, of course has its attraction. We want desperately to become conscious—"And there was light" (Genesis 1:3). How nice it would be for our egos if we could overcome everything dark and, therefore, also sinister. Our nightmares would disappear. Unfortunately, the myth of the dragon slayer shows only how we can be overwhelmed by illusions. It shows how we cut off a part of our soul, how we kill it and push it even farther into the dark and the unconscious. Killing the dragon also means to overcome fear and anxiety. Sören Kierkegaard writes justifiably, "The one who has learned to fear, has learned what is most important!"

The one-sidedness of a mythological image can function dangerously or destructively, especially when only the positive is emphasized. To be sure there are also mythologies which stress the negative above all. About one hundred and fifty years ago, children were perceived as diabolical creatures, as beings ruled by the Devil which had to be literally beaten out of them. Many children were beaten to death in the attempt to conquer the devil in them. I am reminded of the story of Meretlein in the novel *Green Henry*, by the Swiss writer, Gottfried Keller. The negative mythological image of the devilish child can be as harmful as its counterpart, the poor, innocent child who is abused by its parents.

We find the phenomenon of a one-sided mythological image again and again in feminine figures of mythology. For more than two thousand years, mankind has repeatedly suppressed the demonic side of the feminine. The image of Mary, the Mother of God, has just as harmful an effect in its purity and freedom from sin as does the mythologem of the dragon slayer. For Mary's sexuality to be ignored in our image of her is bad enough. Far more devastating, however, is the attempt to repress all aggressive, destructive qualities of the feminine. "Mary saves us from Satan's cunning," writes Conrad Ferdinand Meyer.

Because it is so one-sided, the "nice," positive and pleasant image of the feminine results in problematic consequences. We often hear statements such as, "If women ruled the world, if all mothers came together, there would be no more war, no armed conflict among nations or between different political parties." Virginia Woolf, for one, was passionately convinced that all armed struggles could be seen as the result of masculine aggressivity. In other words, femininity is the same as peace-loving, an image which corresponds to that of the Mother of God. If we no longer recognize the aggressive, destructive side of the feminine, if we repress those aspects, then we are incapable of accurately evaluating and understanding the true feminine. I would like to simply point out from Greek mythology that Aphrodite was the beloved of Ares, the god of war. We can recall how overjoyed the Olympian gods were when they saw the two of them caught together in the net, the trap set for them by Apollo.

I would like to return to our topic of the benevolent father by way of summary. I am fascinated by the mythological background for the notion that a solely benevolent father is supposedly necessary for the healthy development of a child. The myth is the same as that of the natural sciences which explain and rule the world by means of the law of cause and effect, allied with the mythological image that Good leads to Good and Evil to Evil. All of this, of course, is further combined with the dragon slayer, a myth that has its origin in Christ and his victory over Satan. I must say this mythological cocktail leaves a bad taste in my mouth. The *admixture* of mythological themes can only lead to an infantilizing of human beings. If we swallow this potion, we remain children forever, never becoming responsible for our neuroses or our own destructive sides. All of our difficult and negative characteristics can be blamed on father and mother while we, ourselves, are completely innocent.

At the risk of seeming repetitious, I would like once more to take issue with causality, to point out its detrimental results, and to give psychological reality its rightful place. None of us is "caused" or determined primarily by our parents. The psyche is independent and outside of the law of cause and effect. Although we certainly take on many virtues and vices from our parents and from our environment, we only take on those qualities which most closely correspond to our inherent psychic nature. An example: A man is brutal, beats his children, abuses his wife, and has no feelings. We might well say that this man is the way he is because his mother was cold and his father brutal. But this is not the whole truth. He took from his parents what fit for him. There is no point in blaming his parents, for that would be to avoid his individual responsibility, especially if we are talking about an adult. We do not merely become our parents. There are many, loving individuals who had terrible parents and the other way around. "The strawberry grows underneath the nettle/And wholesome berries thrive and ripen best/ Neighbour'd by fruit of baser quality," says the Bishop of Ely in

Shakespeare's, *Henry V*, (I,1).

As I have stated, it is very difficult not to succumb to the image of causality. Perhaps we should use a different kind of language. H. K. Fierz, a Jungian psychiatrist in Zürich, says, "Jungians are different from other psychologists: they do not speak about cause, but about constellation. Something is constellated, not caused." Nevertheless, how can we practice psychotherapy if we, like Jung, are not led by causality? What if we try to discover reasons for pathology in order to heal? How can we work if we are not inspired by the mythological image that "Good leads to Good and Evil to Evil?" Following this image, we would help our patients to unload their feelings of guilt onto their parents. How are we to understand anything in psychology without causality?

I would like to suggest that as psychotherapists we can only work under the image of the autonomous psyche, never under the image of the dragon slayer or that of causality. As in the case of the patient I described at the beginning of this chapter, her terrible father was a blessing for her. She took from him what he had to offer, the destructive side of the father archetype. She had to find the protective side of the archetype elsewhere which was not at all easy. Still, she blamed no one for her sleeplessness. She accepted the autonomy of her own psyche and, thereby, of the uniqueness of her life.

Psychology, psychotherapy and analysis all have a mythological background. A large part of our therapeutic work is rooted in mythology. We assist our patients in finding the mythic qualities of their lives, in shaping and forming their personal mythology. In psychotherapeutic work lasting months and years, we transform what seems to our patients to be the *massa confusa*. We transform the meaningless chaos of their lives and sufferings into meaningful mythological stories, novels and dramas—into tragedies, yes, into comedies. This transformation of the meaningless into meaningful mythology comprises a part of the healing effect of psychotherapy. An incomprehensible life begins to take on the nature of a biography.

The different schools of psychology provide their patients with different explanations of their suffering. Often as psychotherapists we believe we give our patients causal explanations of their lives. In fact, we only help to discover a mythology that gives their lives some measure of meaning. There is a Freudian mythology, a Kleinian, an Adlerian, a Kohutian, a Jungian and so forth. All of them create an interesting mythological life story out of the random events of the patient's existence.

Psychotherapy and psychology are an art, not a science. From the material at our disposal, dreams, fantasies, feelings and emotions, we practitioners of the art produce fiction, poetry, essays, portraits and pieces of theater. As James Hillman writes, "The curtain rises, the gods make their entrance upon the stage. We know not what happens; we only know that something does happen."

In this chapter I focused on the positive sides of the sinister father. In the one which follows, I will describe a father who rarely is a blessing to his children, namely the important, unusual, creative father.

CHAPTER 3

SONS AND DAUGHTERS
OF UNUSUAL FATHERS

"What loveliness in life for any child
Outweighs a father's fortune and good fame!"
Sophocles, circa 496-406 B.C. *Antigone*, (702-703)

Unusual fathers presuppose usual or ordinary fathers and yet, what is an ordinary father? Every father differs completely from every other father. What qualities, then, do "usual" fathers have in common? And should we not preferably talk about fathers *and* mothers? Or, are daughters and sons of unusual mothers different from those of unusual fathers? How, specifically, does the father function? How the mother?

These and other questions confuse me until I begin to lose the thread of my thoughts. After having practiced psychiatry for decades, even my experience proves itself unexpectedly limited, offering me no support. Seen from the statistical perspective, too, my experience is quite limited. In twenty or thirty years a therapist might see five to ten sons and daughters of unusual fathers. The number might be less since they are just that, unusual and uncommon. The material of my experience hardly suffices to draw authoritative conclusions.

I turned, finally, to mythology, being at the same time aware of the limitations of this approach. For those of us from Western European culture, the Christian and, to some extent, the Judaic mythology is primarily decisive and determining. In Christian mythology we find a family at the very beginning of Christendom. I mean, of course, the Holy Family, the family with the parents, Joseph and Mary, and their son, Jesus. As in every family, we have a father to deal with, namely Joseph, himself almost less than a usual father. In the earthly sense, the first Christian family was completely matriarchal—Joseph did not even beget his child. Mary became pregnant during the couple's engagement—by the Holy Ghost, as she maintained—and good-natured Joseph accepted the illegitimate pregnancy. When Jesus then came into the world, Joseph remained loyal and pleasant, but completely in the background. In all the stories of the birth of Jesus Christ, Mary and her child are, as a rule, the focus of attention. They dominate the "show;" they are worshipped and revered. Somewhere to one side or behind the scenes stands the humble father, Joseph, who is scarcely noticed! Although he organizes the flight into Egypt and the return to Israel, we do not hear much about him in the New Testament accounts afterward and not much more in popular legends.

From the period when Jesus began his ministry at the age of thirty, no mention is made of Joseph. Mary, on the contrary, apparently involved herself in Jesus' activities and on at least one occasion had to be bluntly rebuffed by her son. At the marriage in Cana, Jesus says to her, "Woman, what have you to do with me?" (*John* 2:4) Apparently, she could not help interfering. In the reports of Jesus' death, we find nothing about Joseph, his father. Mary not only is included in the scriptural narrative but later tradition surrounding Jesus' death and resurrection make much of her presence, especially in artists' renderings. Mary with her dead son, Mary, the grieving mother of the vanquished hero, has continually inspired artists anew. Father Joseph, on the other hand, gets completely forgotten: he is of no importance.

Given Joseph's seeming lack of importance, I have a hard time understanding why it is often said that Christianity has shown patriarchal characteristics from its beginnings. The earthly father of the first Christian family barely has any role at all to play—he is simply a supernumerary. I seriously doubt that Joseph, in spite of his insignificant role, felt reassured and strengthened in his self awareness by allusions to the Holy Ghost and a questionable Father in Heaven! Jesus, then, had two fathers: Joseph, a totally unimportant, ordinary, well-meaning carpenter and good provider; and God, as significant and unusual a Father as we might hope to find. At the same time, nothing is more difficult to grasp than this Father God. We can neither see nor touch him. He is hidden—if He exists at all!

Mythologems are simply representations, images and symbols of archetypes, not of individual human beings. All the archetypes can appear and have an effect in any human being, women, men and children. The universality of archetypes allows me here to avoid the question of whether men and women or, in this case, fathers and mothers, are truly different or not. Mary and Joseph are certainly fundamentally different archetypally. Mary is the blessed, beaming Mother of Christ, revered and worshipped. Joseph is the unassuming, ordinary, insignificant, yes, practically superfluous, background figure.

According to Jung, archetypes originally represented classical human situations or arose from such situations. We could also say that classical, human situations are the actualizations of archetypes. Archetypes do not, perhaps, incarnate themselves solely in human beings, but also in life forms related to humans, mammals for example, or even in animals generally. In the case of our cousins, the chimpanzees, the males and females are usually involved in a lively game having to do with the distribution of sexual privileges and power positions. The males are constantly dependent upon the support of the females, whose absence sends them anxiously into hiding in the trees. Aside from mating, the males are dispensable and are used only as a kind of luxurious plaything.

While we can scarcely see birds as related to humans, the peacock illustrates graphically what is at stake. The sole function of the peacock (the male of the species) is to spread his impressive tail to entice the female to mate. The peacock, by the way, made Charles Darwin almost ill — that was how he, himself, expressed it. He saw no possibility of explaining the purposeless luxury of tail-spreading as "Darwinian," that is, as developmental, causal or goal-directed. We might well imagine that the peahen murmured to herself after mating, "He really did not have to flaunt his tail so much!"

As far as humans are concerned, we forget again and again that, from a zoological perspective, the human male, too, is rather superfluous — except for mating. Other women could protect and feed pregnant women. Other women could hunt or gather fruit, be that in a classical or in a modern sense. Among many so-called primitive peoples, not only care of the children, but also the procuring of foodstuffs, the field work and other tasks lay in the hands of the women. The men, on the other hand, palaver, wander about, and now and then involve themselves in often deadly conflicts. The matriarchy of the Holy Family is admittedly rather extreme. The one area where the husband is truly useful and necessary is missing since Mary conceives without Joseph. The luxurious, lustful joys of sexuality for which many women require men was apparently not a concern for Mary.

It may not be a coincidence that women are in charge of 99% of all kindergartens. We need not mention that in elementary and even middle schools, female teachers are in the majority while male teachers are disappearing. Males are scarcely necessary — even if they may be stimulating. In this regard modern developmental psychology is consistent with the existing situation. The mother is the primary one who proffers the good and the bad breast, who mirrors and admires and who forms and influences the determining first years of the child. Most psychologists recognize a certain value in the father's position as "mother's little helper" or as a well-meaning, tolerated nuisance, a variation on "her majesty's loyal opposition." Father does not seem, however, to have a formative function during the crucial beginning period of a child's life.

The ordinary, average father is not only ordinary, but

for the most part, unnecessary. The reader will protest vehemently and contend that it indeed is extremely important for growing children to have a father with whom they can identify or to whom they can relate. The reader might further protest that a father introduces children to life in society. He is someone who plays football with the boys and who frolics in the yard with the girls or admires their pretty dresses. All these things, I would point out, are an added luxury and not essential or necessary no matter how pleasant and entertaining.

I am not here talking about a thoroughly proven scientific explanation, but simply an idea I have. I suspect, as I have intimated, that the ordinary father plays a very minor role in the family and in the life of children. His natural function is that of a luxury article. Nevertheless, is it worthwhile living without luxury? In public life, in business and the like, a man plays the role of male, but not that of father. When rebelling against so-called "male domination," we should, therefore, not speak of "patriarchy" but of *phallocracy*. The Patriarch, the dominating father, is something like a windmill besieged by female Don Quixotes.

Now we come to our actual topic: Unusual men as fathers. There are men of great importance, unusual men, who are also fathers and less innocuous than Joseph. At this point I come up against a wall: what does it mean to be an "important" or "unusual" man? Somehow I have to find some solid criteria for this term "unusual," conscious all the while that such criteria would have limitations. They would be *my* understanding of "unusual."

Most human beings — men and women — are about ninety percent collective beings. As Aristotle noted, man is a *zoon politikon*, a herd animal — naturally also in the positive sense. He does what one does, feels what one feels and so forth. Human life from cradle to grave takes place in the lap of the collective conscious and the collective unconscious. We all share, more or less, the views and attitudes of the ruling collective — or, perhaps, of the ruling oppositional collective. There exist but very few truly original, gifted, creative individuals as I have pointed out in Chapter 1. If we were to examine the views or philosophies of the greater number of our fellow humans, we would discover that they are usually copies of the "Neue Zürcher Zeitung," "New York Times," or the BBC European News. Not that the media creates the collective conscious and unconscious; they simply reflect and reinforce what *is* collective.

There is a collective as well as a counter-collective. Both are collective and the individuals who comprise them lack any individuality and originality. In the field of politics there are those who conform to the right, those who conform to the left, and probably also those who conform to the "middle." All these positions, however, are collective as are practically all of us. I do not mean this in a disparaging way. Man is not God, not a creator, but a creation. If I look upon a field of narcissuses, I do not ask of each narcissus to be especially original. The field filled with flowers gives me pleasure just the way it is with all its unoriginal blossoms.

From time to time, though, there are unusual individuals — in our case, men — who demonstrate independent, creative capabilities, be it in the arts, science or in business. Here I would like to propose a further thesis: such individuals as fathers are, as a rule, a misfortune for their children. Mary Wollstonecraft, a courageous English feminist of the eighteenth century, quoted with delight the words of Francis Bacon, the English philosopher (1561-1626), "Wives and children of great men can only be victims, hostages of destiny." By "great," Bacon understood "self-determining, powerful, unusual, original, out of place."

Truly original, powerfully creative talents usually require so much psychic energy that there is not much left over for other human concerns. Recently, I heard from a famous German critic whose name unfortunately escapes me. He commented that all good authors and writers are actually egotistical, inconsiderate, narcissistic monsters, only interested in themselves — except when they work creatively in their own fields. The mythologem from the Judaeo-Christian tradition presents an even grimmer picture. I am thinking of the powerful story of Abraham and Isaac. Abraham, of course, was one of history's greatest creative figures, founding and creating the people of Israel according to

God's special command. And what did this same Abraham almost do with his son, Isaac? He received the order to sacrifice Isaac, to slaughter and burn him and he would have carried out the order had not God, Himself, intervened. Although I am limiting myself for the most part to the Judaeo-Christian mythology, I will here insert a slight deviation. Another significant man, Agamemnon, commander of the Greek armies in the Trojan war, sacrificed his daughter, Iphigenia, to ensure the success of the Greek forces.

Drawing from mythology, it almost seems as if genuinely creative, original and significant men not only sacrifice many parts of their psyches, but also have the tendency to sacrifice and destroy their offspring. We find a suggestion of this in the story of the Holy Family. Father Joseph, the ordinary, insignificant man, was a "good Joe," according to all legends and reports, who never harmed anyone. The other Father of Christ, God, was not so harmless: He sacrificed His own son. God sacrificed His Son for His purposes, His plans, albeit for the salvation of mankind as He claimed. Even so, He still allowed His Son to die miserably, crucified between two criminals. The insignificant father never did Christ any harm at all. Christ's significant Father — more significant than God can no one be — let His Son die alone and abandoned.

Unusual Fathers as Curse

These, then, are my theses: First, fathers as ordinary fathers are and remain peripheral figures; second, unusual fathers are extremely dangerous for their children precisely because they *are* unusual. It lies in the nature of the unusual man to be brutal and ruthless toward his fellow human beings. As a father he may even suffer from the compulsion to sacrifice his children!

Let us now translate the mythological images into concrete situations of the sons and daughters of such fathers. We want to investigate whether we can confirm the images to some extent in the actual lives of everyday people. (Of course, even here we are dealing only with partial mythology.) The following may be instructive. Since unusual human beings, as the term suggests, are unusual, and therefore rare, the probability is great that an unusual father will have an ordinary son or an ordinary daughter. An unusual son or daughter might be the equal of an unusual father. Their abilities would generally be coupled with the brutality I have described. They would thus find it possible to hold their own with their fathers and to differentiate and develop their unusualness.

What, though, would happen to the ordinary daughter or the ordinary son of an unusual father? The situation is somewhat different for sons than it is for daughters. The classical mythologem for sons is the story of Goethe's son, who supposedly committed suicide. The ordinary son cannot overcome the unusual father; he cannot achieve the latter's greatness. He must, therefore, feel like a failure all his life, since he will constantly compare himself to his father. Often he will have to seek escape downwards, that is, voluntarily throwing himself into failure. I have noticed how sons of truly significant men frequently fail in every respect—socially, domestically, and professionally—at least at the beginning. The only possibility they have is to move into an area with which their father has no connection, an area which precludes all comparison with their father's activity. One of Freud's sons, for instance, became an engineer. The so-called "killing of the father" is much more difficult for the ordinary son of an unusual father—the father is too impressive, too powerful. The son cannot carry out the necessary "killing" since he runs the danger of coming out the loser in the murderous struggle.

Due to the mythological insight that significant fathers have a tendency to sacrifice their children, I have reviewed several case histories. It struck me how the sons—and daughters—of significant fathers are often subject to actual destructive pressure from their fathers. It struck me, too, how these fathers, not formally or consciously yet in their practical behavior, did everything to destroy their sons especially. To some extent, this showed itself in very small, noteworthy details. One such unusual, creative and extraordinary father who was fairly well-to-do, repeatedly called his twenty-year-old son's attention to men's trousers on sale. Since the son's appearance was unbecoming anyway, this had the result that his appearance was marred even further by poorly tailored slacks. Or, the son of a writer told me how he would proudly show his father a composition that turned out well only to have his father say, "Oh, but this is obviously just a first draft. I am sure the final version will be all right."

The situation is somewhat different for daughters. As I observed earlier, a man has a peripheral existence anyway, not being completely "necessary" but more of a luxury. For this reason he is existentially more uncertain, more readily annihilated. A woman has more of a central position, being much more important than a man for the propagation of the species and existentially more secure. An ordinary man can maybe offset this uncertainty. He may compensate a sense of his limited usefulness for the preservation of his kind through assiduous activity. His uncertainty, however, remains. The ordinary daughter with the greater certainty of a woman can allow herself to be overpowered by her unusual father without herself being annihilated.

We are familiar with many daughters of significant fathers who dedicated their lives to attending to their father's legacy without, themselves, suffering complete ruin as individuals. We might think of Anna Freud whose life consisted of carrying on the life's work of her powerful father. Literature provides us with further examples of daughters who continued in the legacy of their fathers, like Thomas Mann's daughter. Naturally, it is also true that a daughter can hold her own against her father when she is as gifted and extraordinary as he is. Even when this is not the case, she stands a better chance of making her mark in life than a son. At the same time, these extraordinary fathers will tend toward sacrificing daughters as well. Iphigenia, Agamemnon's daughter, reminds us that daughters, too, can fall victim to the unusual father.

In yet another way, the life of children of ordinary fathers is significantly easier than that of children of unusual fathers. This occurs in the area I refer to as psychic self-sufficiency. Case reports of analysis often demonstrate how sons and daughters individuate, how they acquire this psychic quality. Dreams, for instance, show how the collective father can be overcome and the individual subsequently liberated. Dreams show the old king, the collective, beheaded perhaps or some similar image. Among themselves, Jungians often talk disdainfully about the collective Judaeo-Christian, patriarchal attitudes from which the individuating child must free itself. I find this portrayal questionable at best. Earlier I stated that almost all human beings are and remain completely embedded in the collective. In this sense, most children—in or out of analysis—do not free themselves from the collective. They do not become self-determining individuals, but simply adapt to a new collective, the collective of their generation. Psychologically, they just shift from one collective to another one.

On one hand, collective consciousness and the collective unconscious contain contents which remain similar over centuries. On the other, these contents change constantly, producing new characteristics with each new generation. The father or the parents usually represent the old collective. What we refer to as becoming self-sufficient consists then merely of a child's turning from the old to the new collective, a misperception of true self-sufficiency. This step of turning from the old to the new is far easier with a usual father. The old collective is always much weaker than the new and, lacking a strong champion in the "old" father, can generally be overcome effortlessly.

The situation is very different with an unusual father who, almost by definition, is non-collective, original, powerful and creative. Even though his ideas and concepts age with time, they were more original to begin with and, to a degree, remain so. His work, too, while not necessarily having lasting value, is still significantly greater than that of others. The child will have much difficulty pitting him- or herself against such a father. Not only will the child have to overcome the old, antiquated collective in the person of the father, but also powerful, original creations. The unoriginal, uncreative child is, in this sense, no match for the unusual father. He or she will be deeply impressed by the father throughout life, lagging behind his ideas and concepts and therefore will never be completely free.

Unusual fathers, then, are nothing less than a curse for sons and daughters. It is to be wished for everyone that they have an ordinary father, one who is but a peripheral figure existentially. Fortunately, the majority of fathers are ordinary, pleasant men without unusual creative abilities and, therefore, thoroughly bearable and pleasant for their children. They may even provide something additional—they may be a welcome luxury even if not completely necessary. Most of us have benevolent fathers. Only a few children must struggle with extraordinary fathers, those with the tendency to harm or sacrifice their children. We would wish from the depths of our hearts for every child not to have an unusual father, but merely an inspiring "luxury item."

Children of unusual fathers, I should note, are not completely lost. Should they succeed in surviving their fathers, they have proven that they, too, are "someone." This means that they have not succumbed to being social failures, to having to grapple with themselves as shadow existences in chronic depression or to experiencing themselves as completely worthless. Sons, especially, who manage to see their unusual fathers as enriching rather than annihilating, have achieved a level of individuation which, in itself, is most unusual.

Whether we talk about sinister fathers or unusual and ordinary fathers, we cannot overlook the paradox in the nature of the relationship between fathers and children. Yet another phenomenon pertains to the relationship between fathers or father figures and children. This is an area more complicated than it might first appear: the sexual abuse of children. This will be the theme of the next chapter.

CHAPTER 4

MYTH AND REALITY OF SEXUAL ABUSE OF CHILDREN

"Sexual abuse of children is not a psychological phenomenon, but a crime." Audience comment during a lecture on child abuse, 1990

In my thirty-five year practice of psychiatry, I have often had to deal with sexually abused children as well as with adults who were sexually abused during their childhood. I have also done many psychiatric evaluations of perpetrators of sexual abuse. Because the phenomenon of sexual crimes against children has become increasingly the focus of public attention in the last few years, I decided to give a lecture on the topic. To this end I reviewed older as well as more recent literature to better understand the scope of the problem.

The literature, however, proved to be extremely confusing. Some authors assume that more than half of all children have been sexually abused and have suffered considerable psychological trauma as a result. Others, though, are of the opinion that the number of children involved is smaller, maybe 5 to 15 percent. The majority of authors were not precise in their definition of sexual abuse. Some considered abuse to be practically any erotic contact between an adult and a child, ranging from an all-too-friendly pat on the shoulder by a not-so-pleasant uncle to brutal rape. Others did not differentiate hair-raising cases of sexual abuse of two- to six-year-old children from sexual experiences of girls and boys over fifteen with adults. More contemporary authors tend to view any kind of sexually colored experience of a child with an adult as extremely harmful, while others question this perspective. When we examine the different statistics more closely, we find that a third of all cases referred to as child abuse are experiences with exhibitionists. Does every encounter with an exhibitionist truly harm a girl or boy of, say, twelve years of age?

At the beginning of my lecture on child abuse, I stressed the importance of careful study of the phenomenon itself. I emphasized that I would first approach the material "objectively" and "scientifically" and only later would I draw my conclusions. My approach aroused strong protest from the audience. Several women yelled at me and called me degenerate. They pointed out that we were talking about *crimes* and not a "phenomenon" that we might carefully study at our leisure. Any type of sexual involvement of an adult with a child, regardless of the circumstances, had to be treated as a horrible offense. Correspondingly, the only proper reaction would be the most irate indignation. Farther on in the lecture, I mentioned that we really should study perpetrators more extensively to understand the drives and motives behind their actions. At this point several women left the lecture hall under protest after having accused me of identifying with these disgusting criminals.

I later talked to various women who had experienced incest during their childhood. Several had extremely radical points of view. One of them made this comment. "If you chance to look through a window in the evening and see a father kissing his six-year-old on the cheek as he puts the child to bed, you should immediately call the police and the juvenile authorities. Everything possible must be done to at least temporarily separate this man from his family." Others even insisted that every man was suspect as a possible perpetrator and rapist. They went so far as to intimate that a mother should never leave children alone in the house with their father. They considered that even the most apparently harmless man could sexually abuse his children.

Following the lecture and discussion, I spent a few days in Great Britain and had a chance to read the local newspapers. I came across reports of satanic rituals, of pedophiles who sacrificed and killed children. The newspapers described how, during demonic rituals, children were forced to watch fearful tortures of other children to intimidate them and to make them submissive for every kind of sexual abuse. Each article stressed in closing that until now the police had found no evidence for such awful activities. The reports also quoted several psychologists as saying that reliable patients had admitted having been the victims of satanic rituals as children. Many patients of course had temporarily forgotten these horrible events, but had again remembered them in the course of extended psychotherapy.

Reading these newspapers reminded me of the history of the Order of Templars which I had studied in high school. This order of knights was founded in 1119 A.D. to protect pilgrims on their way to Jerusalem. For various reasons, including their considerable holdings, the Templars became unpopular and aroused suspicion. In the year 1305, they were charged with heresy, but, more to our topic, they were also accused of sexual crimes. They were said to be homosexual and to abuse small boys—now and then girls as well—and further accused of indulging in satanic rituals. The order was dissolved. Some of its members were burned at the stake and their possessions confiscated.

From the Knights Templar my thoughts went to my studies of Jewish history. I remembered how, during the Middle Ages, Jews were frequently accused of abducting Christian children, of killing them and sacrificing them to an evil God. Whenever such rumors spread, pogroms followed shortly in their wake and many Jews were killed.

Remembering these antecedents, it seems to me that sexual abuse of children encompasses more than at first meets the eye. It has to do primarily with the concrete activities against children which I meet so often in my psychiatric practice. Today these tragic occurrences are very much in the public eye. In addition to the actual concrete events, we are also dealing with collective psychological phenomena which are in some way linked to sexual offenses against children. These phenomena are difficult to describe. They have to do with the psychological attitudes of the collective as well as those of the individual's conscious and unconscious. In other words, they have to do with the individual, with society and a combination of the two at the same time. As I have pointed out in Chapter 2, whenever we are dealing with a theme which is a focus of public attention, we have to examine it on two different levels. We first need to look at the phenomenon itself, which interests us. We also have to consider the psychological background of the individuals and the society which have taken an interest in the theme in question.

In this chapter I will address the actual phenomenon of child abuse less, and will attempt, rather, to determine primarily what this phenomenon arouses in us, what needs it fulfills, and what it constellates in us psychologically. In Chapter 2, I talked about causality and how it applies to the natural sciences but not to psychology. The psyche, at least insofar as Jungians understand it, is acausal and not determined mainly by the law of cause and effect. Psyche is autonomous. Naturally, psychology cannot completely neglect causality, but must understand it as a symbolic image of relationship, of connection. Children, for instance, connect with their parents. Education and the social environment play a major role in the formation of individual character and provide a backdrop that can lead to very different results. I mean to emphasize that what we term "causes" can have widely differing effects. A lack of love from the environment may result in retarded development with one child, while for another, such lack might serve as a creative challenge (see Chapter 2).

We all need causality. Everything that happens frightens us a little less so long as we believe we have discovered the cause. Our knowledge of cause, we hope, will enable us to influence events, nature and human behavior. It may even make us capable of healing the latter. Interestingly enough, nothing has stimulated psychological mythology so much as our need for causality. Although, as I have already mentioned, causality bears limited significance for the field of psychology. Due to our search for causes of human behavior, of suffering and joy, we have created innumerable psychological myths in the last hundred years. Unfortunately, we have operated under the mis-apprehension that the myths themselves were the real causes! I referred in an earlier chapter to the fact that masturbation was viewed for decades as the cause of all possible kinds of psycho-logical disturbances. At that time people attempted to prevent the practice by tying boys' hands during the night or by electri-fying small boys' penises as a well-meaning deterrent. Today we recognize, of course, the mythological nature of notions re-garding the negative effects of masturbation.

More and more of late, we have come to view the cause of many developmental problems in individual psychology as stemming from sexual abuse in childhood. Some specialists go so far as to assume that more than 90% of all cases of anorexia and bulimia can be traced to such abuse. They thereby satisfy our need to identify a cause for these puzzling disturbances. Psychological mythologies which identify something extremely awful as the cause of neurotic and even psychotic disturbances seem to particularly attract us, a point I discussed in an earlier chapter. A reprehensible and disgusting "cause" gives us the strength to combat it, to direct our indignation against it. Since sexual abuse of children is completely evil and totally immoral, it satisfies our moral needs as well.

The mythology that revolves around sexual abuse of children offers us more than the gratification of our needs for causes and for morality. We live today in a transitional period from patriarchy to matriarchy, a transition which has already occurred in many areas of our lives. While men still dominate the fields of politics, business and industry, they have already lost countless battles. The majority of families have a matriarchal structure in which the men have less and less of a voice. Sexual abuse of children provides us not only with the "cause" of most problematic psychological development — an evil cause at that — but with the villain: a man. The evil patriarchy thereby becomes the source of practically all psychological difficulties, of all the sufferings of human kind. It represents the male beast who almost incidentally abuses children sexually whenever the opportunity presents itself.

The net of mythology, weaving itself around the all-too-real sexual abuse of children and gratifying our longing for causality, meets many of our needs. The benefits we derive from this mythologizing make it very difficult to investigate and judge the phenomenon proper to appropriately deal with it. Frequently, a crusading zeal overpowers us, making us enthusiastic champions against the powers of evil. The crusade mentality helps us understand why I aroused so much indignation during my lecture by insisting on the need for a close study of sexual abuse. Clearly, child abuse is wrong and criminal. Our task is to combat this evil and to eradicate it, not to waste time in careful observation or in collecting evidence!

The mythology surrounding child abuse has other aspects. Earlier I mentioned the discussions I had with women whose childhood was overshadowed by incest. Some of these women had frightful stories to tell. They suffered indescribably at the hands of their fathers or of father figures as well as from the apathy and neglect of their mothers. Other "incest survivors" had relatively harmless stories to tell. One related how a teacher had kept a fourteen-year-old girl after school to help her with her homework. As he sat beside her, he tenderly stroked her hair or her back. Or, an older male cousin regaled younger children with obscene jokes. Or, a stepfather inspected a fifteen-year-old girl with lecherous glances as she dressed for a dance. Regardless of the details of the stories, the effect of the experiences for most of the women was that they felt deeply wounded. For the most part, they hated their fathers or father figures intensely. Many believed that there should be no statute of limitations for sexual crimes.

Most of these women were intelligent, sensitive and pleasant to be with. Their hate for their fathers, though, was so profound that I had to ask myself if it were not an almost religious emotion? All of us are misused and mistreated children in some way or other, sexually or otherwise. We are all "abused," especially, I might add, by God the Father. Life, itself, can be terrible through no fault of our own. Illness besets us; physical deformities threaten us; misfortunes of all kinds frighten us. Our Heavenly Father mistreats us over and over without our being able to understand the why's and wherefore's. I feel that it is most unfortunate that we use "father" as a symbol for God and most particularly disadvantageous for actual, human fathers. I began to ask myself whether at least some of these women were not actually wrestling with God. Confusing their actual fathers with God Almighty, they held their concrete fathers responsible for all the evil in the world.

Sexuality is usually connected with love. Even in cases of sexual child abuse, affectionate, loving feelings frequently play a role between perpetrator and victim. Could there be a better image of the relationship between God and Man? God mistreats us continuously while He apparently loves us at the same time. Perhaps these women are grappling not so much with God as they are with Satan, the dark side of God, and his representatives in this world. At the beginning of this chapter, I mentioned rumors of satanic rituals involving children who were sacrificed or at least frightened to the point that they no longer resisted. Now I ask myself: Behind the range of powerful reactions toward child abuse, is not the child archetype at work, an archetype which is much richer and more varied than we generally realize? A child is always more than Little Johnny or Little Mary. In every child we experience one or more aspects of the archetype of the child which express themselves in many symbols.

One of these symbols is the divine child which we find in many religious traditions, especially in Christianity. Child Jesus is born in a manger in Bethlehem. He heralds a new era and a new kind of humanity, even promising the salvation of the whole human race. Whenever something new appears capable of redeeming us individually and collectively, it is often represented and experienced through the symbol of the divine child. Yet whenever the divine child appears, its archetypal opposite also emerges: the destroyer of the child, the child killer. When Herod learned of the birth of Jesus, he had all children of the same age killed in the hope of destroying Jesus as well. The divine child, the hope of the world, and the child killer, Herod, are both symbolic representations of the archetype of the child.

We can identify still other aspects of the child archetype. We often refer to ourselves as "children of God." This is another image of the child archetype which expresses our relationship to God and our relationship to the devil who sacrifices children. The image of Mary, the good mother, belongs to the child as well. It should not surprise us, therefore, that schools of psychology ruled by the child archetype lay such importance upon mother. For them the role of mother is so central that they go to the extreme of insisting that analysis temporarily replace the good mother. Yet another side of the archetype—and this *is* surprising—is the direct connection between child and our concept of "divine causality." The divine child presents a possible "cause" for our salvation and its destruction would mean the end of all our hopes. The archetype of the child even includes aspects of the war between the sexes. Jesus, one image of the divine child, originated as an earthly being solely from Mary. Joseph, Mary's husband, did not beget the child. If God were to become female, as the feminist theologians demand, then the divine child would have no male parent at all—it would have descended entirely from the feminine!

The child is such a powerful and many-sided archetypal symbol that we do not wonder at the relative impossibility of differentiating between "clinical facts" and projected mythological stories and images. Child psychologists hold the opinion that children never lie when it comes to sexual abuse. At the same time, we frequently observe children unjustly accusing adults, particularly under pressure from one of the parents in divorce cases. Mythologically, however, the child who only tells the truth is an accurate image: the divine child is innocent, truthful and incapable of lying.

One way we can view the work of psychotherapy is as allowing mythological images to take effect. Mythology, psychological mythology, leads and directs us. We may not, however, overlook the character and quality of this mythology given the great influence it has on our therapeutic activity. Not all mythologies are healthy. Some are sick, deformed, one-sided and, under certain circumstances, might be harmful.

It was James Hillman who, several years ago in Rome, pointed out that classical psychotherapy has its basis primarily in the mythology of the child archetype. Hillman suspects that the mythology of the child, which dominates psychotherapy, very often leads to an unintentional and undesirable infantilizing of the patient. Psychotherapy *can* make him or her incapable of becoming a responsible, adult citizen. Patients remain or become children, continually complaining about Mommy and Daddy and blaming their parents for their woes. Hillman felt so disgusted by the damaging effects of the one-sided domination of the mythology of the child that he stopped seeing clients. He declared further that psychotherapy is immoral. Hillman's position is clearly a case of throwing out the baby with the bath water. Nevertheless, he has helped us to reflect more about the nature of the mythology which guides our work and to what degree it might be helpful or harmful. This is one of the reasons why I have chosen to address the mythological aspect of our interest in the sexual abuse of children.

The mythological net surrounding the concrete abuse of children is an extremely one-sided mythology of the child. It is the mythology of the neglected child, a near relative to the mythology of the victim. What I call good, healthy mythologies — if I might use such a banal term — include the most diverse sides of an archetype, especially its polarities. We can understand archetypes, at least partially, as polar. Consequently, we often meet them as oppositional images: man and woman, puer and senex, parent and child, God and Satan, heaven and earth, Aphrodite and Ares, wounded/healer, Jesus and Herod, victim and perpetrator. Hillman certainly has grounds enough to protest over the extent to which the child archetype rules our work. While certainly a rich and many-faceted archetype, the child is but one of many which might give our work its stamp. The situation becomes much worse when we only use a part of the child archetype or some of its split off fragments.

Let me recapitulate. Sexual abuse of children is frequent and atrocious and must be combated with all available means. The interest shown by lay and professional persons for this dark side of childhood may well help us to do more by way of prevention. In addition, it is our duty to study the mythological/psychological background of the current interest in this phenomenon. What need of ours does this interest fulfill? What kind of mythology stimulates our fascination with the phenomenon? To what good or bad end do the mythologies lead?

One of the mythologies behind the contemporary interest in the sexual abuse of children is, as I have already stated, the mono-polar, or one-sided myth of the innocent, neglected child and victim. This myth can do harm and, almost secondarily, can impede our ability to study the facts. During the lecture I mentioned earlier, I stated that in large cities—and doubtless also in rural areas as well—most girls and boys have met with exhibitionists on occasion. I further commented that I was not completely certain whether such experiences caused such great harm. The audience protested passionately: the aroused masculine member presented to view by these exhibitionists had wounded these innocent girls most profoundly. The subject was not a matter for discussion or investigation.

I also commented in my lecture that, as far as I could remember and to the extent I could today observe, most boys are approached or molested by a homosexual some time during their childhood. The adult might be a male cousin, an uncle, a neighbor or an unknown man. As far as I can tell, these homosexual encounters do not always cause great psychological damage. As a rule, boys discuss such occasions with great interest among themselves. Because of my position on this question, several women in the audience denounced me as perverse. These innocent children had encountered the Devil—an unpleasant, obtrusive man, that is—and had therefore been severely harmed. I even dared to question whether, in fact, every encounter with a sexually importunate adult is necessarily severely harmful to the child. My question raised the suspicion that I was a "male chauvinist pig."

The one-sided, unipolar or split-off mythology of the innocent child and victim even has the capacity to hinder our therapeutic work with sexually abused children—or adults. The manner and method many therapists use to deal with the guilt feelings of "abuse" victims amply demonstrates my point. Children who experience sexual abuse often feel guilty. They have the impression that they, somehow, were at fault. Older children, in particular, have ambivalent feelings about the abuse. They are uncertain whether the experience did not provide them with a certain pleasure. They often wonder if they failed to defend themselves or possibly encouraged the perpetrator. Many psychologists reject these guilt feelings out of hand as completely unjustified. They maintain that in no way can there be a question of guilt. They encourage children to forget the guilt, to put it out of their minds.

This therapeutic position can be harmful for the psychological development of a child. Therapists simply think of and accept the child as a victim. They energetically reject and deny any attempt on the child's part to assume any responsibility for what happened or at least to recognize his or her own ambivalence. Therapists thereby impose a victim psychology upon the child, a psychology which says that for everything that happens there is always someone to blame. They nip in the bud the child's growing awareness that he is at least partially responsible for much that happens to him—or at least for the back and forth tension between rejection and acceptance. This therapeutic position does not take the child seriously as a human being. It sees the child solely as a mistreated, innocent victim. The child is no longer a part of creation with all its possibilities and contradictions, with its conflicting instincts and desires.

One area where contradictions and conflicts surface is the relationship between the child and the perpetrator. The perpetrators are seldom strangers. They are usually men—less frequently women—who have a relationship of some kind to the child, if not as father, then as uncle, cousin, or neighbor. A third person may discover the abuse, but the discovery generally results from something the child intimates or says. For this reason, the child may feel like he has betrayed the adult. The betrayal is naturally all the more painful the more closely related the child is to the perpetrator—a more or less loved stepfather or the actual father.

Experts and specialists in abuse cases advise

psychotherapists to help these children to forget any feeling of betrayal. Psychotherapists thus fall under the domination of the one-sided mythological image of the pure, innocent child and victim. They do not honor the actual psychological situation, and this is truly tragic. The children are caught in a conflict of loyalties—loyalty to themselves on one side and loyalty to individuals who are close to them on the other. A child has to accuse his father, for instance, even though by so doing he betrays someone whom he perhaps deeply loves.

These children suffer from a conflict that no one can resolve. Psychotherapy should help them to tolerate and endure this tragic conflict. Such assistance would help them to mature. Conflicts continually burden human lives, be it those of adults or children, conflicts that are simply tragic and cannot be resolved. Ideally, psychotherapists would assist their clients, whether adults or children, to bear these conflicts and to grow and develop through them. When we treat sexually abused children as if they were incapable of tolerating the tragedy of life, we rob them of a specifically human potential. We also wrong them by not taking them seriously as human beings and treating them as one-sided archetypal symbols.

The situation is much the same in the treatment of perpetrators. Many of those who abuse children would have us believe that they loved the children but that they expressed their love too physically. Many professionals who work with children experience a certain physical attraction to their charges. Otherwise, they would not be able to stand the continual contact with them. Thus it happens that teachers, for example, who in some mild form have made advances to their pupils, are often very good teachers and demonstrate genuine love for the children. Such perpetrators defend their capacity for love energetically and feel themselves unjustly attacked. When we treat perpetrators we often make two basic mistakes due to our one-sided mythology. On one hand we represent what they have done as only bad. We try to convince them that they are degenerates and that a complete change of their character is absolutely necessary. We see them as the Devil incarnate and want them to share our perception. On the other hand, (and this is much worse,) we force them into the victim role. We tell them we know that most men and women who abuse children suffered abuse themselves as children. They are not, therefore, truly responsible for their deeds since their actions were the result of the abuse which they, themselves, suffered. In taking this approach, we repress the archetypal polarity. We do not treat these people as human beings who are always partially victim and partially perpetrator and, for this reason, are always responsible to a certain degree for whatever happens to them.

The unhealthy mythology which often directs our interest and our relationship to child sexual abuse has other consequences. I mentioned at the beginning of this chapter that a part of this mythology consists of our belief that we have discovered the Devil incarnate. We begin to believe we have found the root of all evil, the very origin of human neurotic and psychotic development. This belief can make us into fanatical missionaries. In my capacity as supervising analyst, I continually meet psychotherapists who hunt for traumatic sexual events in the childhood of their clients with a certain fanaticism. Should a client relate a dream in which incest occurs, the psychotherapist seizes the opportunity with great enthusiasm to thoroughly question the patient on whether he or she can recall any sexual harassment or violations during childhood. Often the patient remembers nothing. The psychotherapist, however, assumes that something of this nature must have happened. I have experienced cases in which the client fabricated a traumatic sexual event from childhood simply to please the therapist.

Psychology is neither mathematics nor physics but mythology. We can only understand and grasp the soul through symbolic images and mythological narratives. While these images and mythologies are collective, the mixture of images and mythologies that direct us personally is something very individual. We need, therefore, to be conscious of the images or mythologies that affect us personally in our work.

Here I would like to make a parenthetical comment. In the last few years our culture has considerably demystified sexuality. It has lost much of the mystical, demonic character which it still possessed, for example, when physicians considered masturbation the source of most psychological confusion. I sometimes ask myself whether the "sexuality-is-completely-natural" attitude is only the result of a powerful repression and suppression of the demonic side of sexuality. We have shoved the demonic aspects of sexuality into a corner and see them only in the "demonizing" of sexual abuse of children. As I mentioned, many people consider any encounter with an exhibitionist extremely damaging and they automatically label as evil every sexually colored encounter a child has with an adult, regardless of the circumstances.

Besides the mythological background I have already presented, I ask myself whether another mythological theme is not involved. I am thinking of the myth of the family and those who accept it or reject it. The family is a small unit which holds together. It frequently defends and shields itself with all possible measures against the outside. Families tend to protect their terrible, their destructive and their creative secrets. Even today, most children grow up in families, and families profoundly influence children's development and attitudes toward life. This small unit is a place where tenderness grows and love blossoms on one side and where, on the other, uncontrolled brutality, misuse of power, and frequently, fear reigns.

It seems that many individuals who care deeply for the happiness and healthy development of other human beings get angry about this small, secret-harboring unit. Neither the State nor the public nor social workers nor teachers can look in on the family. No one may interfere with it. These well-meaning individuals have a collective social vision. Their desire is for competent specialists to determine all aspects of life. They would like to see all children cared for primarily by trained educators and, for this reason, they believe that children should begin school as soon as they can. When the famed American educator, J. Dewey was asked what the best age was for children to start school, he responded, "A child should go to school as early as possible." Psychologists and educators who share Dewey's position would like organizations of specialists to control all aspects of society. Furthermore, they would like for these secret-harboring units, these perverse families, to give up their power.

This is the mythology of complete professionalism, a professionalism that should have the final say in everything. Professionals should teach children to play (play therapy), should assume the instruction in sexuality (sex education), and should teach children how to make use of their free time.

This myth of the professional joins itself to the one-sided mythology of the child. In its rudimentary form, the family is a whole, a unit, a developed, responsible organism. As such, it includes everything: responsibility and irresponsibility; love and hate; loyalty and betrayal; maturity and immaturity; good and evil. According to the myth of the professional, the priests of professionalism must divide and rule this whole, complete organism. They must undermine it and infantilize it. They must turn it into an irresponsible, helpless, childish institution. Their motto is, "Parents are the only individuals who are not, under any circumstances, capable of raising their children."

Naturally, sexual child abuse happens very frequently within this secret-harboring circle of the family. I suspect that the deep desire to break the power of the family often strengthens the enthusiasm for the struggle against sexual abuse. Just turn the care and education of children over to professionals, to the priests of humanity's infantilizing!

All archetypes are always with us and in us. Some are more in the foreground and dominate; others are weaker and more in the background. The ego does not determine which archetype rules from one minute to the next, but it determines the movement and the development of the collective unconscious. This is the case whether we are talking about psychologists or laymen. The mythological images and symbols which guide us never represent all the archetypes at one time. They may consist of one-sided, unipolar images of split archetypes. The one-sided images are not all that harmful. What may be harmful is for us not to be conscious of the whole or split archetypes ruling us at any given moment. Another detrimental factor is the taking of our limited and one-sided mythologies as concrete fact. We see ourselves and others through the eyes of the ruling archetype, represented by the mythological images. When we misunderstand this necessarily narrow perspective as the whole truth, we begin to see ourselves and others as distortions.

I have nothing against modern psychotherapists following the lead of the archetype of the child. Why should we not trace every neurosis and every psychosis back to certain traumatic experiences in childhood? Why should we not see a bad mother or an incapable father as the source of psychological suffering? We should go ahead and let ourselves be ruled by one-sided images. We should let ourselves be ruled by the image of the innocent divine child and by Herod, the murderer of children. We should be ruled by Satan, who sacrifices children, or by the cause of all causes, the wounding we have inflicted on the divine child. We will still remain competent psychologists as long as we do not assume that we are talking about facts. We can still function effectively if we do not believe that the "facts" we observe have nothing to do with our personal psychological background and archetypal situation.

Naturally, all archetypes act internally as well as externally for us, whether as wholes or as split off fragments. This is why we so easily fall victim to concretism and psychological narrowness, why we see our archetypal situation only outside ourselves and project left and right. The dominion of the child archetype has its disadvantages to be sure. To be ruled, however, by the split archetype of the child without being aware of it can truly endanger our work most severely, no matter how good our intentions. When we split the archetype of the child and identify with the divine child, we unconsciously fall into the other side of the archetype: the child abuser or murder. This is the paradox of the phenomenon of child abuse. In the next chapter I will focus on a particularly extreme form of psychological paradox.

CHAPTER 5

THE BLESSINGS OF VIOLENCE

"God hates violence." Euripedes, *"Helena,"* 1, 412

Violence burdens humanity like a curse, poisoning the lives of individuals and families, religious and political groupings, peoples and nations. The paradoxes and contradictions I have presented through many examples in this book seem at first not to apply to our experience of violence. Most of us assume that violence is clearly wrong; but is it really?

I will begin with personal illustrations and examples for the theses which I will discuss later. This is a way of proceeding that lacks a certain logic, but in this context will be meaningful.

When I was six years old, there was a small square surrounded by several small houses close to my parent's house. It was an ideal place for children to play. A girl of about ten who lived in one of these houses was the uncontested ruler of the square, refusing to allow other children from the neighborhood to play there. If any dared to enter the square, she drove them away with considerable brutality. I, too, was shut out of this lovely play ground. As I returned home one day, once again saddened by the situation, a newspaper delivery woman asked why I was so downcast, and I poured out my troubles to her. She replied, "Little one, you are wearing wooden shoes" (a practice still widespread at the time). "Just do this. March into the square, go up to that little girl and let her have a couple of hefty kicks in the shins with your wooden shoes. You'll see! She won't bother you anymore." With a certain naivete, I turned back, entered the square in question, approached the girl and gave her two powerful kicks in the shins with my wooden shoes. She howled loudly and fled in tears into her parents' house. From then on, she left all the children alone who wanted to play in the square. The spell had been broken. Following my deed, I felt good and was pleased with myself. In a manner of speaking, I had done something positive for myself and the other deprived children, but I had also satisfied my malevolence, my childish pleasure in violence!

Here is another personal story. The teacher of the third elementary school class that I attended when I was nine was vicious and mean. He especially had it in for children from poor backgrounds and treated them cruelly, even striking them. One little boy in particular, named Jurg, he hit brutally with a ruler for the slightest offense. One day, when this vicious teacher again headed for Jurg to hit him with the ruler, the victim lost his nerve. Jurg jumped out of his chair and tried to get away. The teacher ran after him, but the little boy was escaped, screaming as he ran from the classroom. About fifteen minutes later the door opened and a stately, elderly woman entered the room. She was the victim's grandmother, a washerwoman by profession, with whom Jurg lived. With her face flushed red, she marched up to the teacher and thundered at him, "Mr. H., if you hit my Jurg one more time I will beat you left and right about the ears until you don't even know your own name." The teacher stammered something about discipline and bringing charges and the woman left the classroom. The brutal teacher never again hit Jurg and behaved somewhat more cautiously toward the rest of us students as well.

Here is another story. As a medical student, I had what

we called the underdog position, junior resident in a small psychiatric clinic. On Tuesdays and Fridays we administered electroshock therapy, often on the advice of the charge nurse or someone comparable. If one of the patients had called a nurse or one of the other staff a derogatory name like "fool," they considered him dangerous, aggressive or depressive and absolutely in need of treatment with electroshock. In those days, EST was a very brutal, therapeutic measure in many clinics. The patients were extremely afraid of it and resisted with everything they had at their disposal until we were able to press the little button and they lost consciousness from the epilepsy-like seizure. Another resident and I administered these treatments with a feeling of pronounced horror, but with the conviction that it was therapeutically necessary. Today we question whether such brutal methods actually helped the patient. In any case, they disturbed us as medical students deeply. One of my colleagues even cried the first time he had to administer EST.

Now a story that is not one of my own. Several weeks ago I read the following article in a British daily newspaper. Two fifteen-year-old girls attending the same high school had been at odds with each other for a long time. One of the girls spread the rumor that the other one was pregnant. During a break between classes it came to a confrontation. The supposedly pregnant girl (she was not, in actuality) had brought a kitchen knife with her to school. She intercepted her tormentor and threatened to stab her if she did not immediately stop spreading rumors about her. Her rival refused to take back her comments while the gathered students called out, "Just stab her! We don't have time to wait for you to work up enough courage to do something." The first girl grasped the knife, stabbed her rival and killed her. Thereupon, she ran home crying.

By way of conclusion I want to mention a statistic. By the age of eighteen, most Americans — and, I assume, the majority of Europeans — are said to have witnessed tens of thousands of murders and acts of violence on television alone.

That violence in some form accompanies and fascinates us in our lives is clear to each of us. When we talk of violence, however, we have to differentiate the various forms it takes.

Physical, bodily violence is the use of physical means to force, manipulate or torture someone. *Psychological, mental* violence, on the other hand, is just as important and certainly occurs more frequently than physical violence, but it is not as dramatic and not as likely to appear under the rubric of "accident" or "crime." Against our wills, we humans are forced to do or to not do. This occurs through threats of the withdrawal of love or of blackmail, for instance. It also occurs through the activation of a guilty conscience, of anxiety or of psychological confusion. We may simply be psychologically mistreated and tortured.

I remember a girl of about sixteen, who was completely under the power of her mother. Her mother became instantly "ill" at the slightest difference of opinion. "Mother doesn't feel very well; see what you have done to her," the submissive father would accuse the overly-conscientious daughter from time to time. I also remember the five-year-old boy who came home from kindergarten crying in despair. It turned out that the kindergarten teacher had staged an ugly psychological game with the children. On the blackboard she wrote the names of those who most wanted to sit by whom. Naturally, it became apparent that no one wanted to sit next to this particular boy. The teacher underlined the name of this unfortunate and said to him, "See! That is you! That's your name! What's the matter with you that no one wants to sit by you? You have to change. Obviously no one in the class likes you."

Children and adults alike can be tortured just as much with psychological means as they can with physical brutality. Psychological violence is no less sinister and destructive than physical violence. Humans are physical *and* psychological beings. Our abilities are of both a physical and psychological nature and, therefore, we can express violence both physically and psychologically. Human relationships are always, regardless of how much love is present, a power struggle at the same time. This is the case whether we are talking about the relationship between boyfriend and girlfriend, between men and women in general, or between two people in a marriage. Violence, especially psychological violence, plays a major role as a weapon in power struggles in all relationships, sometimes more, sometimes less.

Wherever we look, no form of violence is new. Not violence between individuals and groups, peoples and nations, or as a means of maintaining order within societies and states. The resolution of individual and collective power struggles by violent means characterizes the history of humanity. The phenomenon of violence has continually accompanied the human race up to the present. Not only has it accompanied our species, but it has fascinated us as well. Even advocates of all that is good and beautiful, like Bernard Shaw and Sartre and other Western intellectuals, marveled at the atrocities of Stalin. Not only for intellectuals, but also for the majority of humans, pure, pointless violence, violence for its own sake, exerts a tremendous attraction.

Our conscious attitude toward violence, of course, varies and has varied greatly. We find one extreme in Christianity, the complete rejection of violence—". . . But if any one strikes you on the right cheek, turn to him the other also" (*Matt.* 5:39), or ". . . for all who take the sword will perish by the sword" (*Matt.* 26:52). All the same, did Jesus not use violence to drive the moneychangers from the temple? Is it not interesting, too, that we can not find violence on the list of the seven deadly sins?

The other extreme is the repeated glorification of violence. One example is Homer's descriptions of the battles around Troy in which he rendered the struggles of the heroes with dedication and enthusiasm. These battles often ended in death for one or the other. We know countless tales of battles from the Middle Ages, how the hearts of the onlookers beat faster at the sight: "Glorious to witness how the heroes exchange blows and the way the blood flows." In Shakespeare's, "*Henry V*," the Archbishop of Canterbury says:

> "Whiles his most mighty father on a hill
> Stood smiling to behold his lion's whelp
> Forage in the blood of French nobility." (I, ii)

Praise of violence also fills more contemporary literature such as Ernst Junger's *The Storm of Steel and Battle as Inner Experience*.

Contemporary "brutalo-videos," which many adolescents are practically addicted to, carry realistic presentation of violence to extremes: skulls are squashed, limbs severed and everything else equally or more disgusting. Even people not directly confronted with violence in their daily lives watch these kinds of films over and over again. Any one of us who should happen to turn on the television will generally see someone shot or beaten within five minutes. Although more civilized in their form, sports, too, present us with violence, ritualized though it may be, especially football, rugby, boxing and wrestling.

We human beings are not alone in our propensity for violence. Nature, the Creation, itself—and thereby also the Creator, God—are characterized by brutality. Eat or be eaten, destroy or be destroyed, in order to survive. Nature's violence, in addition, appears as the completely pointless violence of natural catastrophes or outbreaks of epidemics. Until just recently, most human beings experienced Nature as threatening and sinister due to the quality of its violence. In the Middle Ages only the mentally deranged loved the Alps with their thundering avalanches and hurtling rocks. The beautiful, peaceful landscapes which today provide us with our Sunday strolls are, as a rule, creations of man and not of the Creator. In truly natural landscapes, we would sink in bogs, fall into chasms, be bitten by snakes or buried by rock slides. Contrary to our image of it, Nature is not characterized by peaceful harmony, but by what we might call chronic acts of violence. It seems that even whales and dolphins do not plow peacefully through the high seas in blissful harmony, but engage in bitter struggles with one another.

The ingenious and unbelievably complicated mechanisms of creation impress us repeatedly, just as Nature moves us with her apparent beauty. Only anesthetized sentimentalism could bring us to overlook the violent and brutal occurrences amid the "naturalness." In 1755, an earthquake almost totally destroyed the city of Lisbon. The leading minds of Europe's age of Enlightenment asked in their shock, "How can we continue to respect a God Who commits such offenses against His creation?" Since this creation is so brutal, must we not conclude that the Creator is equally brutal? I will return to this question a

little later. In any event, man as a creature of this violent Creator, made in his violent image, resorts repeatedly to violence
as a means of asserting himself and out of sheer pleasure. I do
not find it useful to view man's brutality solely as an expression
of pathology, as a psychological or sociological maladjustment.
We must assume that violence belongs to the essence of man as
a creature—a profoundly disturbing notion for us!

The theory of archetypes is one of the fundamental
concepts of Jungian Psychology. We Jungians assume that the
human psyche does not issue from a single mold, but results
from many different psyches, forces or psychoid aspects, what
we call archetypes. From a Jungian perspective, then, how are
we to classify human violence? Is our tendency toward and our
pleasure in brutality a force in itself, an archetype, or merely
part of some other archetype? The complete rejection of violence
by Christianity and by many modern individuals is thoroughly
understandable. (Pacifists, at least in Europe, are for the most
part heirs of the Christian tradition, even if their rejection of
violence does not rest upon religious beliefs.) By definition,
violence is above all something purely destructive. Through
violence, be it physical or psychological, we "force" another
creature, a living being, human or animal, to behave differently
than it would like or chose to behave. We thereby destroy a part
of their being; we block the realization of an other's intentions,
wishes and efforts. Violence always carries destruction.

How might we Jungians understand the archetypal
significance of violence? Does violence belong archetypally to
the shadow? Of course, by "shadow" I do not simply mean
everything that lies in shadowy places, whatever we are not
conscious of. I do not mean, as is so often the case when
"shadow" is addressed, whatever we individually and
collectively reject for the most widely differing reasons. I do not
mean anything that does not correspond with our ego ideal. The
archetypal shadow is that which, according to Jung, is totally
destructive, the murderer and self-murderer in us. We also need
to realize that, without the shadow, man would be soulless, with
no consciousness of any kind. Only those who can say "no" to
creation are capable of saying "yes" to it. Wolfgang Giegerich

touched on this point in a 1991 lecture at Lindau ("Killings: Violence from the Soul"). He suggested that we regard the pointless killing of animals, their wholesale slaughter, as a sacrificial act, as the moment of birth of the human soul.

In Freud's language we would refer to the shadow as *Thanatos*. In his book, *Beyond the Pleasure Principle*, Freud describes two fundamental instincts of human life, *Eros* and *Thanatos. Eros* serves to promote life, one's own and that of others, while *Thanatos* seeks to destroy it. The archetypal shadow, therefore, would be related to *Thanatos*, the death instinct, regardless of whether this instinct were conscious or not. The conscious archetypal shadow, the killer and self-killer in each of us, is just as active, sinister and uncontrollable as the unconscious one.

Since violence strives for destruction, it could well have to do with the archetypal shadow, which would explain why violence seems to be inherent in human nature. The equation, violence equals archetypal shadow, does not completely prove out, however. If we prevent a child from running across a busy street by using violence, we are certainly not acting in the interests of destruction. On the contrary, we are using violence out of love. Perhaps violence is something like a Germanic mercenary in the Roman Empire. The mercenary soldiers would represent split off parts of the shadow, helpful when properly applied, but ready at any time to murder and plunder. The question is, "What makes the difference?" I would propose that we need to differentiate between violence *with Eros* and violence *without Eros*.

We are often driven to do things which harm ourselves or others, whether we do so out of ignorance or destructiveness. More commonly, though, we are divided in our intentions and our efforts. We are ambivalent, pulled back and forth so to speak between *Eros* and *Thanatos*. What we want or what drives us is not always to our benefit. Often our fellow human beings support our positive intentions through physical or psychological violence while repressing the negative ones by the same means — to our well-being and wholeness! Many are those rescued from ruin not by gentle persuasion, but by physical or psychological force. It is certainly desirable and beneficial to protect others from violence with counter-violence. When we see a woman assaulted on the street, it is right for us to throw ourselves on her attacker and to prevent him with force from carrying out his criminal intent. It would certainly be false to simply stand by and only attempt verbally to dissuade the attacker from further violence.

We can use force or violence in the service of Eros or, stated in plainer terms, in the service of the individual human being or the human community. We can also use violence in the service of the destructive, the malicious, of the archetypal shadow, the murderer and self-murderer in each of us. This latter use of violence can have terrible consequences. There are certain individuals whose relationship with Eros is extremely weak while their relationship with Thanatos, with the archetypal shadow, is quite strong. Several decades ago, psychiatrists applied the term "psychopath," or "moral insanity," to such cases. The why's and wherefore's of this phenomenon of moral deficiency have not been established and, perhaps, never will be. The fact of the matter is that there exist individuals who direct their efforts primarily toward the annihilation of those around them if not themselves. The more destruction they encounter or they can cause, the better. I remember that Saddam Hussein beamed as he announced on Iraqi television, "The entire Middle East will become an inferno."

Such psychopaths can wreak terrible havoc using violence unscrupulously as they do for destructive ends, regardless of whether they are business leaders, politicians, dictators or criminals. Since they have no scruples, no one else is a match for them. Their goals are unequivocal because they do not suffer from morality's ambivalence. Their energies are concentrated and focused. It is something of a miracle that psychopaths are not the primary rulers of humanity, for they hesitate at nothing in the selection of their methods. Fortunately, it appears that in the long run, there are always individual human beings and peoples who dare to defend themselves with violence — the violence that they deeply mistrust — while trusting in *Eros*. When psychopaths dominate specific areas of human activity, they can be held in check to some extent with the help of law and order. When, on the other hand, they have achieved positions as leaders of nations, it is difficult to know how to deal with them. Those of us who are peace-loving are caught on the horns of a tragic dilemma. Should we allow ourselves to be conquered, dominated or destroyed? Or should we resort to force to defend ourselves and run the risk of being destroyed anyway?

I would like to come back to a reference from Christianity cited earlier: "All who take the sword will perish by the sword" (*Matt.* 26:52). The use of force, as this saying suggests, leads to escalation on a collective and an individual level. Nowhere is violence something neutral. It is not an energy or an instrument which we can employ without danger. The danger is present even when our intentions are good, our relationship to *Eros* strong and our purpose the preservation of our lives or those of others. Seen psychologically, violence is a force in itself, perhaps, as I have suggested, very similar to the archetypal shadow. *Of itself* it seeks to destroy — even when destruction can sometimes work to the good. If violence is not identical to the archetypal shadow, it at least appeals to the archetypal shadow in us. Whenever we resort to violence, including for the service of *Eros*, we are invoking our destructive side, what I call the murderer and self-murderer in us.

The first two stories that I told — the story of the girl whom I kicked with my wooden shoes and the one of the tortured boy's grandmother — are clearly examples of the use of force *with Eros.* The feeling that I had when I kicked the girl in the shin was not only a concern for my fellow human beings, but also a certain pleasure in causing her pain. I do not know what the grandmother's feelings were when she threatened to box the teacher's ears. Hers was a noble deed: she used force out of her sense of *Eros.* At the same time, she perhaps also took pleasure in humiliating the teacher.

The psychological situation with the other resident and myself when we administered electroshock therapy was much more complicated and horrible. We had learned that EST was therapeutically useful. On the other hand, we completely saw through the need for punishment and the brutality of the head nurse and chief orderly. We also saw through our pleasure in brutality toward the patients, even though we attempted to balance it out with our caring attendance before, during and after the administration of the treatments. Above all, the medical indication justified this pleasure, this enjoyment of brutality, although we, of course, recognized that it was questionable.

The story of the school girl who stabbed her classmate is an instance of violence without any *Eros,* of violence as the expression of the destructive, archetypal shadow. This applies as well to the ideologically or religiously tinged and murderous activities of Genghis Khan, Robespierre, Hitler, Franco, Stalin, Mao Tse-tung, Saddam Hussein and other criminals of world history and their cohorts.

As I noted earlier, brutality, the brutal characteristic of human beings, is closely related to the archetypal shadow in us or, at the least, is its cousin. We cannot embellish this kinship away. We have to look this terrible fact in the eye whenever we consider how and when and if at all we should employ violence. Because brutality is at least related to the archetypal shadow, we can readily grasp why many individuals warn against violence in principle. We can also understand those who go so far as to envision the possibility of a world devoid of violence. That kind of world is probably not possible, since as an archetype, the Shadow belongs to the nature of human beings, as we know it today. It belongs to any nature which continuously attempts to be aware of itself. The use of psychological and physical violence, whether individually or collectively, always means that we avail ourselves of the destructive. For that reason, the danger constantly exists that destruction will take control, even if we originally intended to use violence only in the service of Eros. Nevertheless, the danger does not excuse us from having to muster the courage to employ violence with Eros when the need arises — as a blessing, in other words.

This question is not an abstract, intellectual dalliance, but a very concrete problem. We cannot imagine, for example, a modern nation without a well-organized police force. Naturally, the police can only function when they are willing in certain cases to use violence to protect citizens against crime and criminals. To use force in this manner is to play with the murderer and self-murderer in us. Ideally, then, a policeman should be someone who is prepared to engage in such play, to approach the murderer and self-murderer in himself and to use it for the well-being of the community. He must engage his brutality to serve *Eros* without allowing himself to ever be controlled by this archetype.

I would here like to address the problem of those who object to and of those who volunteer for military service. We can certainly find brawlers and Rambos among the volunteers and among the conscientious objectors, genuine pacifists operating out of their idealism. (We can begin to grasp their pacifism when we recognize the awfulness of violence!) Many military volunteers are just as peace-loving or more peace-loving than the conscientious objectors. They accept the risk of exposing themselves to the deeply terrifying force of violence for the public good. Volunteers for military service are often tremendously idealistic, sacrificing much time and energy for something that is awful and unpleasant for them. Among the conscientious objectors there are many who are close to violence and, for *this* reason, object to doing military service. How often have I heard them say while I was giving them their physical examinations, "I don't know what I might do if I had a loaded gun in my hands. I would probably shoot down the first person I saw!"

My view of brutality as an unalterable characteristic of human beings may seem pessimistic. I do not truly believe that the lion and the lamb will ever live in peaceful harmony on this earth. I will go a step further. The real brutality in this world comes from God (insofar as He exists) or from the gods. No one is as brutal as He. As a rule, God and the gods are characterized as brutal. Only as the belief in God (and the gods) gradually lost its strength and reality did man begin to think of God primarily as "loving:" "God is love, again I say, God is love." Anyone who could say this has not experienced God. Almost all religions describe their deities as terrifying, brutal and awful. This could hardly be otherwise since the creation, nature and man (with his claim to being made in God's image), is itself brutal.

I assume that an encounter with God or with the transcendent, per se, can only then occur when we experience the violent side of God, creation and mankind as well. We meet God and the world just as much in the horrific as in the beautiful and sublime. We meet God just as much in thunder and lightning as in a breathtaking sunset, as much in natural catastrophes as in a romantic, idyllic landscape. To experience the love of God, the friendly, nondestructive side of creation and mankind, is easy and pleasant, requiring little of us. The true *Auseinandersetzung* with God and the world takes place only when we face God's brutality and through it come somehow closer to Him.

I have to follow the last statement with a warning: In no way do I intend to glorify violence. To glorify violence is to evade the terrible. Violence, the second cousin of the archetypal shadow, *is* terrible, terrible and horrid, collectively as well as in individual cases. We can only glorify it by minimizing it, thereby denying its demonic nature. I would emphasize, therefore, the following: Violence belongs to God; it belongs to creation and to humanity. This is very difficult for us to accept, just as it is also difficult to recognize, accept and consciously experience our archetypal shadow. Often we attempt to evade this difficulty by seeking causes for mankind's brutality. Specific causes and contexts of a psychological, sociological, political, economic, religious and cultural nature certainly exist. Violence in itself, however, *has* no cause. Violence is an essential attribute of humanity, related to our archetypal shadow, our murderer and self-murderer.

This brings me to a very delicate question which I have not considered until now. I am almost afraid to address the issue, namely, the question of the relationship of violence to gender. Is violence, perhaps, not really something human, but something masculine, a result of the Patriarchy? Are men, as we know them from the Patriarchy, violent, while women are peace-loving? Is "the Masculine" per se, violent and "the Feminine" peaceable, nonviolent? This is a theory that we hear now and again and one which I have already mentioned. According to this theory, when the Patriarchy has been overcome and the Feminine (or women) reign, war and violence of all kinds will end or at least be diminished. Are women truly nonviolent or less violent in comparison to men?

We can answer the question, "Yes and no." I have pointed out that there are two varieties of violence, physical and psychological. It is the case—and we do not know why—that over the past thousands of years of human history, men have been physically stronger than women. What could be more natural than men, due to their physical strength, having a tendency toward physical violence and having a preference for this form of violence in dealings with women and other men. In any event, in the war of the sexes, there would not have been much point for women to have relied on physical violence. Men clearly have had the advantage. For this reason, men maintained and still maintain their domination and power by physical violence.

Until recently, most of the European countries guaranteed physical violence toward women legally: a husband had the legal right to beat his wife. In this century, particularly in the last several decades, physical strength has lost its importance more and more, playing an increasingly smaller role in relationships. Technology has made it gradually superfluous. It has been dethroned, so to speak, in everyday life, at work and thus also in relations between genders. For my part, I do not believe that rape and abuse of women is on the increase; they are simply more the focus of public attention. They are an atavism since the use of physical violence itself is atavistic.

In the area of sexuality, physical force plays an important role for men. Not only can the man dominate the woman by his physical strength, but from a purely anatomical perspective, the man can more readily assert his sexual desires than a woman can. A woman cannot force a man to have intercourse, not because of a disparity in physical strength but because of anatomical differences. Until now, women have been much more at the mercy of men's sexual desires than the other way around. This does not mean that women are not just as violent as men. Nature—God—has limited women in terms of physical and sexual violence and, therefore, they probably have developed the art of psychological violence more fully than we men. The more that bodily strength loses significance—is no longer "in"—

the more women will be victorious in the battle of the sexes, at least for the time being.

As nearly as I can tell, women often enjoy a superiority over men in he use of psychological violence. There are certainly as many men who have been severely wounded psychologically by women — mothers, wives, lovers, daughters — as there are women who have suffered damage from physical violence by men. I am not just pulling this statement out of my hat. I have observed time and again that, in milieus in which physical violence still plays an important role (among blue-collar workers, for instance), the men often are not afraid of their wives, but more the reverse. The less bodily strength, physical violence, is accepted, the less the milieu values these qualities, the more men appear to fear their wives. I have observed over and over how upper middle-class men scarcely dare to even defend themselves against their wives' demands. If we were to examine marriages more closely and become better acquainted with a greater number, we would clearly recognize that women are just as brutal as the men they live with. Generally the violence is not so much physical in nature, but psychological. By belittling or by sighing at just the right moment, we can often accomplish more than we could with a blow!

We have to take all generalizations with a grain of salt. There are men who understand psychological warfare better than women and many women who are physically more violent than men. Mythologically, goddesses are no less violent than gods. Insofar as gods, goddesses and other mythological figures symbolize what is archetypal, the idea of the absence of violence in women is difficult to support. We might think of the war-loving and battle-happy Amazons or the Gorgons, Medusa, for example, whose very glance was lethal. We might recall Kali, the bone-festooned ruler of the place of skulls in whose honor hundreds of goats were slaughtered and who drank blood from a human skull. We might remember Ta Urt of Egypt, lion, crocodile and woman, devouring and death-dealing, or Hathor, the goddess of war, or Morigan, the Celtic goddess, who is represented as a corpse-consuming crow.

The situation in Christianity is somewhat confusing since

we worship what we consider to be a "masculine" God. (Despite her ascension into heaven, Mary is not truly a goddess.) Our Christian God, I would suggest, is violent not because He is "masculine," but because He is divine. Even were we to pray, "Our Mother, Which art in heaven," instead of "Our Father...," we would still have to confront the terrible, brutal aspects of the Deity.

It seems to me that violence is not something that has anything to do with masculine or feminine: only the nature of the violence has to do with gender. I do understand, however, why it is often said that violence is solely a masculine phenomenon. We would like to be able to localize violence so as not to have to confront its reality, so as to maintain the illusion that we might eliminate the cause of violence. If brutality is a universal human phenomenon, even a divine phenomenon, we have no choice but to face it. We have little hope that it will simply go away. We should not, therefore, attempt to minimize violence by localizing it causally. Dealing with violence consists of having the courage to recognize that as human beings we are violent, that we tend toward violence and that we could not live without violence. In this regard Americans are more honest. They have a saying: "Violence is as American as apple pie." Yet, violence is not just American. It is human, belonging to male and female, proper to children and adults, not even stopping short of old age.

As psychologists we are often not terribly courageous in the confrontation with violence. We attempt to avoid the main issue through the use of Latin terminology such as "aggression" or "the inhibition of aggression." Aggression is a neutral concept, an abstract term with a Latin root and means simply "to approach something, to grasp something." It is not the pleasure in grasping that is problematic for us in human nature. Problematic is that humans are violent in the sense that we at times derive pleasure from thwarting and shattering the intentions of our fellow beings. We can apply violence constructively or we can fall victim to it. Are we psychotherapists not in danger of abusing violence? Expressed more moderately, does not our psychological understanding provide us with methods for psychological violence all too ready at hand?

I mentioned earlier that I differentiate between physical and psychological violence. In the course of this chapter I have also emphasized that psychological violence has become increasingly important in the relationships between individuals. Correspondingly, physical strength and, with it, the use of physical violence has decreased in significance. As psychologists we are also specialists in psychological manipulation. We always manipulate our patients and our fellow human beings a little, whether we want to or not. Ideally, we psychotherapists, as specialists in psychological violence, use our ability with *Eros*, with love, in the service of humanity. There is always the danger that we will use the psychological violence inherent in our knowledge of the psyche not with Eros, but out of the archetypal shadow. Thus psychotherapists are as capable of terrible harm as they are of tremendous good.

What of the *blessings* of violence, which I have been tracking in the context of seeking out everything paradoxical in psychology? For a long time I looked for such blessings, but could not find any. I recognized only that when we use violence with Eros it is always very dangerous, even if it could be applied constructively. Then it finally came to me. To grow and develop psychologically we have to confront the entirety of our humanity. This is most difficult in relationship to the archetypal shadow, the murderer and self-murderer in us. This shadow is admittedly most specifically human. I would point out that he who can not say "No" to creation is also not capable of saying "Yes." As Wolfgang Giegerich says, if man had never killed an animal merely for the sake of killing, he would not be the creature that he is today. At the same time, it is infinitely difficult, if not impossible, to approach this terrible archetype, the Shadow, to experience it and to confront it.

Many Jungians, to be sure, talk about the need for the integration of the shadow. How are we to "integrate" the murderer/self-murderer? Yet this is the direction in which we might find the blessings of violence. Using violence in the name of *Eros* allows us to experience, even to live out, the archetypal shadow without causing too much harm. Every time we employ either physical or psychological violence, we experience our pleasure in destruction, we experience our destructive shadow. We are able to live it out, but, if we are fortunate, not to destroy.

Violence *is* a blessing if we have the courage to employ it under the banner of *Eros*. At the same time, we have to admit to ourselves that this use of violence animates some of the deepest layers of our psyches. When this happens, we meet our murderer and self-murderer. We have to confront the archetypal shadow. For psychological and religious reasons, we have to see and to experience the terrifying in ourselves, the world and God, even if we find the experience awful. Here we can learn from violence. Even though it is horrible, through violence with *Eros* we have the necessary opportunity to experience the horrible.

> *"Being scared is man's best friend.*
> *No matter how the world enhances*
> *the feeling Moved he feels the monster deeply"*[1]
> Johann Wolfgang v. Goethe

People continually accuse us psychologists of living in an ivory tower. They say we attend to individuals but neglect our duty as citizens, that we have no interest for the polis. For this reason I will turn to the subject of politics in the next chapter even though it is not my area of specialization.

[1]*"Das Schaudern ist des Menschen bester Teil, Wie auch die Welt ihm das Gefuehl verteure, Ergriffen fuehlt er tief das Ungeheure."*

CHAPTER 6

THE FELICITOUS REVIVAL OF NATIONALISM IN EUROPE

"The hateful mask has fallen, man remains without scepter, free, unconfined, only man, equal, classless, belonging to no tribe or nation, freed from revenge, worship, title, king over himself, just, gentle, wise."
Percy Bysshe Shelley, 1792-1822

"Nationalism is a form of incest, is our idolatry, our delusion. Patriotism is its cult."
Erich Fromm, 1955

In the last few years we have experienced major changes in Europe. A powerful, deluded system has collapsed. This system not only had dominated the peoples of Eastern Europe, but had also found admirers in the West, despite the bloody excesses to which literally millions fell prey. No one can say for certain what caused this collapse. Inevitably, though, we have to ask ourselves whether one reason might have been the unshakable *Nationalism* of the Poles and the other eastern European nationalities.

For more than ten years the Poles struggled against the basis of the delusional system and, since defeat of their resistance was impossible, the deterioration of the system began. Strongholds and forward positions alike fell like dominoes and, toward the end, even East Germany collapsed. The initial Polish assault—we will stay with the Poles for the moment—was impressive, their tenacity toward the omnipotent system astonishing. The fall of the last domino—East Germany—was still somewhat unbelievable: twelve years of National Socialism of the worst kind, forty-five years of Communism practiced with German thoroughness and *now* democracy and capitalism! How could this happen?

The destruction of the Berlin Wall was not the major historical event. More so was the resistance of the Polish dock workers in Danzig under Walesa. Before and after the first World War, the concept "Mass Psychology," coined by French psychologist Gustave le Bon, was highly respected and widely applied. People understood "mass" as an entity independent of the individual. This assessment, though, became stuck in the negative. The behavior of the masses came to be understood as something terrible, one-sidedly dangerous, as behavior of a faceless beast. We in Europe—and people everywhere—repeatedly experienced powerful, collective phenomena, partly regrettable, partly felicitous: National Socialism, Communism, religious fundamentalism and, in this particular case, Nationalism *a la Pologne*.

What does psychology have to offer us here by way of understanding? What does it have to say about these collective, social, national and international movements? Less than we might expect! Adlerian Individual Psychology, for example, considers the need for community in human beings extremely important and emphasizes that man is a social being, a *zoon politikon*. Ultimately, however, Adlerians view the community above all as the interaction of single individuals, a view which almost all psychological schools today fundamentally share. As a rule, they attempt to grasp the phenomenon of these large, collective movements based on individual psychology. In addition, there are economic, social and political interpretive models for these movements. These, too, rest on a specific conception of the behavior of single individuals. Psychology is knowledge of the soul, which we regard almost exclusively as belonging to single human beings.

Jungian Psychology serves as an exception in this regard, for it has images and concepts for a more inclusive notion of the soul, for a more extensive localization of the soul. In his 1988 Eranos Lecture, Wolfgang Giegerich said, "He [Freud] attached it, psychology, predominantly to the biology of the *individual personality*. Jung led beyond that [thinking] to an unconscious, which as collective and archetypal, no longer has its substrate in the individual human being." In short, we no longer seek the soul only in the individual. The Jungian images and concepts such as, "collective unconscious," "*anthropos*," "*anima mundi*," and "*unus mundus*," express and represent this supra-personal substrate. Are they only overblown words with very different meanings even for Jungians? Let me offer the understanding of one Jungian in the hope of coming somewhat closer to the subject at hand.

The "collective unconscious" we understand on one hand to be what is unconscious or unknown for groups of people and for all of humanity in common. It is like a river flowing through all mankind. On the other hand, the collective unconscious forms a part of the individual soul, which, although similar in all, is found only in the individual. *Anthropos* is Greek for "Man." We assume we are part of this general humanity much as theology assumes that, as Christians, we belong to the body of Christ. At the same time, we also can think of the *anthropos* simply as the image of one human being, carrying within it the individual. *Anima mundi* is the soul of the world, the world soul, of which we are but a part or of which each of us partakes of separately. *Unus mundus*, the one world, refers to the unity of the whole world, a part of which we are, or to an image that each of us as individuals carries in ourselves. We could sum all this up by asking, "Is there an inclusive, greater whole — collective unconscious, *anthropos*, *anima mundi*, *unus mundus* — or is the greater whole only composed of single individuals?" Here we come face to face with the philosophical question of the unity and multiplicity of being.

Romanticism provides one historical example of a perspective of the greater whole. The ideals of Romanticism emphasized unity, a unity which assumed an almost mystical character. Romanticism, for instance, spoke of folk songs, of songs composed not by individual composers, but by the "folk." It spoke of folk tales and folk legends which emerged from the people and were, therefore, a product of the people, not of any single human being. Romanticism even spoke of the "soul of the people," whereby it remained and remains unclear just what that might be. Could there be a substrate of the soul which, as Giegerich says, does not reside solely in the individual? Attributing powers to the soul which go beyond the single human beings is not just a tendency toward a dangerous mysticism—or is it? How are we to understand the following ethnographic incident? Among the Bushmen, the men are often out hunting for days on end. Neither the hunters nor those who remain behind know how long their absence will last. Yet, when the men return to camp, the women have their meals ready. Several hours before the arrival of the hunters, the women have begun to prepare the food.

It seems to me that we should understand mankind not only as a collection of separate beings, but as belonging to something greater, as belonging to the creation, the world, nature and humanity. My concern is not only with myself, but with all human beings; I am somehow connected, I am one, with all my fellow men. We can at least approximate the effect of such psychological realities and forces (represented by the confusing images and concepts mentioned above, like "collective unconscious") with the everyday expression "identification." I take identification to mean the capacity to feel connected to more than just ourselves separately. It is the capacity to derive and to experience our identity not only from ourselves, alone, but finally from the whole of humanity and to act based on this experience. Ideally every man would identify not just with himself but with mankind in general, with the "world soul," with the rain forests of Brazil, for instance. Reality, unfortunately, does not correspond with ideals. Is identification with humanity or even with the environment only a noble, religious or ethical commandment, not a psychological reality? I know no one who actually and genuinely identifies with all humanity. Such a position seems to be in direct contradiction to human nature. As Goethe has observed, "The greatest happiness of the children of man is still only personality."

Let me say a little more regarding this contradiction. Although we feel ourselves to be one with humanity, yes, even with nature in the deeper layers of our souls — something the nice Jungian images express — in practice our identification does not extend so far. All of us, as individuals, are always a part of humanity. While the soul belongs to humanity as a whole (as Jungian Psychology points out!), our conscious as well as our unconscious "identification" is significantly more limited. Remember, by identification I mean our ability to actively identify with something beyond ourselves. We can, to be sure, identify with groups which more or less represent our separate interests as individual egoists. We can identify with groups like the family, a political party, a company, a union, a profession and so forth. Such egoism supported by a group expresses only, and inadequately, those layers of our souls which relate to mankind as a whole.

Let me repeat: Man — and the human soul — is composed of two essential aspects. The first aspect and this is not the most important one, is the individual, the lonely cowboy, so to speak, a "Lone Ranger." This individual occupies the center of today's psychology and has been the central focus of our Western culture since perhaps the beginning of the Christian era. Christianity places greatest emphasis on the individual soul's salvation in contrast to Judaism where God made a covenant with the people, not necessarily with the individual. The second aspect of man is that he is a part of humanity — of the *anthropos* or even the world, of the *anima mundi*, of the *unus mundus* — just as a red blood cell is a part of the human body. While we present, assert and characterize this second aspect as an ethical ideal, we seldom acknowledge its psychological validity.

It belongs to man's overall development that he experience as much as possible all the potentials of his soul, live them out and ideally become conscious of them. In Jungian Psychology we have the concept of individuation. The term denotes the human striving to approximate the meaning of life, to explore the world and one's self in all their depth and to experience and to live out, to sense the divine spark in one's being. The term is misleading. "Individuation" places the individual too much in the foreground, places the emphasis too much on "individual," on "not collective." The goal of individuation is not only the individual, but also humanity. We are accustomed to think of the individual layer of the soul. The layer we designate with the unappealing word "collective," is more difficult for us to grasp, is murkier. The individual is able to identify with himself or with relationships to friends, family and interest groups, but scarcely with his nation or with humanity. That becomes questionable; that is too much. Yet every psychologically healthy individual feels a pressure to identify with a collective, with something greater and not merely with a community of the like-minded (a kind of Mafia), but with a collective that presents a replica of humanity and of humanity's potential.

But I fear we are going in circles. I have to elaborate one point. Individual man realizes his humanity in his own way, a task in which a variety of possibilities and models for living are available. Larger groups of human beings also have greatly differing possibilities for shaping their lives. The Japanese, for example, organize their collective living in other ways than the Americans. The *anthropos*, man as image, the reality of all humanity, is not static. Its very existence depends upon its ability to give form to ever-new expressions of life, not based on changing, outer conditions, but out of itself. We live out these different possibilities of the *anthropos* in smaller groups as well as in our entire race. In other words, the *anthropos* incarnates itself in the individual and in large societies. A "psychologically sound" human being can identify with any group which does not just support his egoism, but offers itself as a symbol, as a representation of all humanity.

Now we come to the question of the "nation." A nation is a kind of group, a community of individuals. This community includes many layers, varieties and variations of human beings—rich, poor, intelligent, gifted, ignorant, mentally retarded, sick and healthy, children and older adults, all kinds of professions from saints to criminals, a replica of the greater human race. This national community is maintained through the activation of certain archetypes, images, ideals and concepts concretized in political, social and cultural institutions as specific forms of life. Individual nations "choose" ideas and images suitable to them from the wealth of the collective soul and allow themselves to be guided primarily by them. (This, of course, does not mean that the images and beliefs of all other nations are absent, just that they are "unconscious.") In terms of universality, the nation symbolically represents all humanity, a variation of the *anthropos*. Yet it does so clearly and specifically enough that the individual can identify with it. Hardly anyone can identify with the whole of humanity. A particular expression of humanity, such as the nation, is a different matter and serves as a symbol for the whole while being only a very specific aspect of human possibilities. I see the nation as a large group of individuals guided consciously and unconsciously by a common fantasy of humanity.

De Gaulle once said, *"La France c'est une idee"* ("France is an idea"), but every nation, not just France, is an "idea." Unfortunately, we grasp this complex reality only in a rudimentary way. We might think, for instance, of the widespread misconception that a common language determines the essence of a nation. While a common language *is* the simplest and most practical fantasy of identity, it is just one among many and is not absolutely essential. The French differentiate themselves from the British not by language, (the French speak a variety of languages), but by life style, not to mention that Basque, Alsatian, Breton, Languedoc and Corsican are all "French" and are all languages which unfortunately are threatened by the confusion of national identity with a unified language. Furthermore, it is not just the French who speak French, but also French Canadians and the Swiss in the western Cantons, among others. West Indians, Americans, Australians, New Zealanders and Irish are very different nationalities and all speak English. Of course, different nations which speak the same language often attempt to give expression to their identity by cultivating different accents or dialects, something which others strangely hold against us Swiss-German.

Each language and each dialect are not only means of communication, but are also expressions of social and collective identity. If the language does not provide that national identity, then identity must find its expression with a variation of the same language. In this regard, the dominant delusion of the "proper" language, the correct, formal version of the language, has been devastating in Europe for centuries. If a Swiss native has to speak "High" German, it is expected of hi — and in a masochistic way he expects it of himself — that he use the same kind of language as a German national would and abstain from any traces of his Helvetian background. Why should he not give voice by a Swiss-German accent to his identity when he speaks? The Swiss accent is neither more appealing nor more distasteful than a "High" German one. It is simply different — it is Swiss!

A part of "nation" as symbol, representative and variant of humanity is — something I have to emphasize — its institutionalization, its governmental organization. The formation of institutions belongs to the essence of man, providing as it does the opportunity for conscious, active involvement with the community. A linguistic community, even a cultural one, does not suffice as a replica of the human race. Both cultural and linguistic groupings lack intentional formation, lack governmental organization. They possess no formal attempt to translate fantasy into structured reality, to actively work toward a common goal with certain sacrifices of energy. Hans Rudolf Baur, an emissary of the Swiss town of Sellenbueren (1805-1877), wrote:"*He who would not for at least a day Render service to the Fatherland without pay, Should in his very soul be of himself ashamed.*"

I think of a nation as a group of people held together, bound by common images, ideas and fantasies regarding the configuration of individual and collective social life. These images must be ones with which the individual can identify, ones which also would symbolically represent the human race. A governmental or at least some institutional form is necessary in order for the citizens to participate and cooperate in as many functions as possible.

I mentioned the ideas, activities, images and the like which serve as an identity for the people of a nation. What do I mean by that? The widely differing factors such as fantasies, around which nations group themselves and thus find their identity, are difficult to grasp and to describe. They are, for the most part, unconscious and often can only be recognized from their consequences. For this reason it is almost impossible to say exactly what is French, what is British, what is Italian or Swiss. Regardless of what it expresses or expressed as a particular piece of folklore, the story of William Tell and the Ruetli Legend reveal the national fantasy of the Swiss Confederacy.

It is difficult to formulate what such stories symbolize. They perhaps symbolize a certain notion of freedom, which had the effect in aristocratic, monarchic Europe of "crude" peasants daring to defeat the noble knights in several battles. As a Venetian envoy wrote in the 17th Century, "A nobleman who fancies himself superior to a peasant will be beaten to death in the Swiss Confederation." Mythology and legend can reflect the basic fantasies as well or as poorly as abstract ideas and slogans like, "*Liberte, Egalite, Fraternite*." Understandably, these central fantasies develop corresponding rituals and formations which are constantly changing.

Fantasies that direct individual nations can only be hinted at indirectly through images, stories and clichés — a circumstance which leads to countless misunderstandings. Single human beings live their own fantasies and possess their own myths while continually misunderstanding each other and themselves — not to mention mutual misrepresentation and projection. The same holds true for nations and their images of themselves and others. This phenomenon makes all more or less well-meaning generalizations laughable: "The Swiss are serious;" "The French are stylish;" "Italians are emotional;" "English are gentlemen" or "The Scots are stingy." It is not a question of characteristics, but of fantasies and mythologies. Even Jung succumbed to this often devastating tendency to characterize nations with specific traits — "the Germans," or worse, "the Germanic peoples are. . . " or "the Italians do such and such."

I see a Nation as a people, organized in a state, supported by a common fantasy and standing as a substitute for humanity. Through the Nation each of us can identify with the human race. Interestingly enough, the most powerful nations of today have very different national fantasies with which they identify. Utopian and religiously colored ideals strongly characterize the United States: equality ("created equal") and the right to happiness and freedom set forth in the *Declaration of Independence*. Groups seeking to establish the ideal State, the New Jerusalem, founded many of the American States. Since the populace of the United States is totally heterogeneous, the fantasy holding Americans together is not one of common origins. Even a common language is not a given for the Americans: English became the national language almost by coincidence. At the establishment of the American republic, only a two-vote majority determined that English, not German, should be recognized as the generally accepted tongue. Today, of course, an ever greater number of citizens of the United States speak Spanish.

Individuals who immigrate to the United States and do not share the American national fantasies often have great difficulties there. (Two of the fantasies about coming to the States are those of seeking an ideal, a better, freer life or of fleeing from persecution and hunger). I once visited a Swiss Club in one of the larger American cities. Most of the Swiss had come to the States to enjoy the fruits of a somewhat higher standard of living. They showed off pictures of their cars and large houses, but, at the same time, were a pitifully sad group. James Hillman, the noted American analyst, once said, "The United States of America is a religion. . . "[1] These Swiss that I met were clearly not communicants of the American faith!

The Japanese have their own national fantasies. Before 1945, one of these fantasies had become national policy and was taken concretely. The emperor was a descendent of the sun goddess and, through him, so, too, were the Japanese people. Half consciously, the effects of this fantasy of divine descent continue into the present. These effects perhaps explain the chauvinism of many Japanese, which often hides behind an

[1] Compare with the similar statement of the historian Carl L. Becker that the American state of Kansas is "'a state of mind,' a religion and a philosophy in one." (Editor's note.)

exaggerated humility. There are other fantasies at work in the Japanese people. One example is the image of the Samurai, the loyal warrior, which today has been transformed into the corporate employee prepared to make any sacrifice for his company. The industrial strength of Japan has partially to do with the Japanese sense of national identity, an identity scarcely broken in spite of their defeat in the second World War.

Common descent is an interesting fantasy, a mythological image of archaic nature. Many tribes and peoples express their identity through myths of origin from common ancestors who are divine, human or animal, like Abraham or Romulus. Adam and Eve are a symbol for the solidarity of humanity in its entirety. I would like to make an aside at this point. Any individual experiences his or her nation, his or her state, as a limitation as well as a source of identity. A national fantasy never corresponds exactly with those of the individual citizens. We could say that the individual citizens' notion of the nation is always somewhat different from those of his fellow countrymen. Thus the national community always exerts limitations upon its members.

I fear, though, that I have neglected the *anima mundi*, the world soul, in my discussion to this point. It, too, contributes to the sense of nation. The *anima mundi* is often connected with the landscapes or particular local topography of a nation: mountains, oceans, plains. The Swiss often long for the mountains, the Scots for the Highlands and so forth. Devotion and love for a nation's landscape are a special identification with the *anima mundi*, but have to do with just a certain part of the earth. Only with difficulty can we identify with the entire earth, with all kinds of landscape. We identify with the earth on the basis of *pars pro toto* (the part for the whole), just as we do with parts of humanity as I discussed earlier.

Identity with the *anima mundi* finds expression in the special relationship to what we call our "native" landscapes. Such landscapes are not necessarily the most beautiful, but nonetheless are "ours," unique parts of the territory of our nation. Through all the centuries during which the Jews were completely dispersed, the image of *erez Israel*, the Land of Israel, played a vital role for them. A territory or parts of a territory are well suited as images of common identity, but are still only images and not necessarily the prerequisite for a nation. We might think of the great spiritual orders of the Middle Ages, the Templars, for instance, as nations without territory. This thought raises the question of the necessity or superfluity of a nation occupying a specific, limited area. While it is certainly easier for a people to inhabit a definite area, it is not essential for the existence of a nation. Essential are the fantasies a people hold in common; to paraphrase *Proverbs* 29:18, "Where there is no fantasy, the people perish" (King James Version). In an age of increasing mobility, we may soon witness the existence of many nations not bound primarily to particular parts of the earth, to a specific expression of the *anima mundi*.

We have, I suspect, lost sight of something: the future of humanity depends upon the ability of a majority of human beings to undertake measures which affect our entire race. Problems have to be solved, which only all humanity is capable of solving: the greenhouse effect, the hole in the ozone layer, dwindling energy sources and other critical ecological situations. Our identification with humanity occurs by way of a symbol like the nation. Since the nation is a symbol of the whole human race, it is capable of effecting measures for the well-being and wholeness of mankind. A world administration governing an amorphous mass of two to four billion people could not effect such measures unless it were composed of saints! Even were that so, the amorphous mass or the uprooted individuals would have nothing with which they could identify. They would sabotage everything and allow themselves to be ruled either by gangsters or by an archaic collective form or by their own, shortsighted egoism.

Does my notion of nationalism seem perhaps too rosy? Why, I might then ask, has "nationalism" become a swear word? What is the reason nationalism has brought so much suffering and strife — do we not have nationalism to "thank" for millions of deaths? Is not the identification with the nation a curse, one under which Europe, alone, has suffered for centuries? Everything human has its pathology and nationalism is no exception. Nationalism's pathology, though, very much depends upon *which* fantasy a nation rallies around. In like manner, pathology in the case of individuals depends upon one's personal myth, whether it be Albert Schweitzer or Al Capone. During their development, many nations succumbed to fantasies of dominion, drawing continuing inspiration from the imperialism of ancient Rome, the *Imperium Romanum*. Ideas of dominion accompanied by commercial interests led to colonial empires, whose character, albeit, depended upon the underlying images. The strength of the fantasy of justice in British notions of dominion resulted in an Africa under British rule being no worse off than it is today. The fantasy of justice even tempered to some slight extent the severity of the Roman Empire!

Imperialism is particularly dangerous for large countries, just as large countries as a rule are much more problematic than smaller ones. At worst, the latter become extremely chauvinistic, take themselves too seriously and value themselves too highly. They are too small to be truly imperialistic. I observed an interesting chauvinistic phenomenon in conjunction with the seven hundredth anniversary of the Swiss Confederation. "We ought not to celebrate," people claimed, "because our hands are dirty." Behind the statement lies the chauvinistic presumption that we, the Swiss, are better than other nations, that we must be more than perfect and exemplary. Were we to require of individuals that they only celebrate their birthdays if they are pure and noble, there would be many fewer birthday parties!

One subject I have not mentioned is racism and anti-Semitism, both of which I consider to be manifestations of nationalism. I see racism as the fantasy of superiority and the attendant right of one group to rule over all others—a kind of genetic delusion of grandeur. One's group of birth determines membership in such a group of individuals. Racism inhibits life and the formation of healthy nations. Because of the racist delusions of the whites, South Africa is not a nation in the sense that I have defined "nation." Any nation uncertain of its identity can fall prey to delusions of racism, for it is one of the enemies of "nation." Due to the same delusional phenomenon, the United States has had to struggle for its identity over the last two hundred years. As I have said, I understand a nation to be a group of individuals gathered around a specific collection of fantasies representing humanity's communal possibilities. A nation, therefore, is open to all human beings. Racism excludes. A black can become Swiss; an Indian can become English; a white — no matter how much he would like to — can never become a black, nor a black a white.

A certain detrimental confusion surrounds the concept of racism, though. Here is one example. During a parents' meeting with teachers, one father pointed out that the situation was becoming very difficult for children who wanted to enter college preparatory schools. Because he noted that sixty-five percent of the children were foreigners with a different mother tongue, he was condemned as a racist. Was he really? I would like to make a few comments on the subject.

Apparently, "racism" means an attitude that rejects the members of other races and overvalues one's own. But what actually is a "race?" Do Italians belong to a different "race" than the Swiss? Or does "race" have primarily to do with skin color? Is a foreigner automatically a member of another race? No one seems to know exactly what a race is. The father in me would like to say, "When individuals of different nations and, therefore, of different national fantasies come together, this can lead to complications. Why can we not simply recognize this fact without immediately becoming suspicious and rejecting all other nations — or races?" If the word "racist" were used in the sense of "nationalist," and if a "nationalist" were simply someone who recognized the phenomenon of national fantasies, it would not be insulting to be labeled a "racist." Why, in fact, do we understand and apply so many words only as caricatures? A "sexist," for instance, is not primarily someone who takes gender seriously and reacts sensibly to it. (An example would be a woman who sensitively registers her own femininity and the masculinity of a man.) Instead, a "sexist" is a man who hates women or a woman who rejects men. We apply the word as a caricature! By such extreme oversimplification, by being *terribles simplificateurs*, we evade every constructive confrontation with confusing social phenomenon. Instead, we use any term relating to these phenomena as invective.

What about anti-Semitism? It would lead us too far astray to thoroughly explore this subject. I also do not feel sufficiently competent to do so. I will, however, say this: All of us, nations as well as individuals, love to have scapegoats. The more uncertain a nation is in its identity, the more it requires a scapegoat for its uneasiness. The less a nation experiences its existence and identity as secure, the more welcome become scapegoats. Poland, continually threatened from outside, has been relatively anti-Semitic, for example. After the first World War, Germany was completely disoriented and succumbed to a deadly anti-Semitism. Great Britain, France, Italy, the Netherlands and Scandinavia have known only a mild anti-Semitism in the modern age, not the deadly variety. These latter peoples are and have been more certain of their national identities, their life styles and their fantasies than, say, the Germans.

Let us return now to imperialism. National or imperialistic fantasies have not caused the greatest catastrophes. It has been *religious* or, I might say, *pseudo-religious* fantasies. I am thinking of delusions which have hardly anything to do with nations, but are usually more supra-national or not national at all. Delusions like these have to be understood as something greater than mass phenomena. When I speak of "mass" here, I mean a group of individuals with an insufficient sense of group or national identity. Religious mass movements present a much greater threat than does a perverted nationalism. They often appear in a population uncertain of its "nationality" or one which simply is not a nation at all. Lacking a nation as a means of identifying with humanity, such populations try to identify with too much at once. Religions connect us with the suprapersonal, with the divine and therein lies their danger. Instead of identifying with humanity through a specifically national fantasy, religious mass movements identify in a grandiose way with God. They purport to know His will and seek to carry — we might say, control — the rest of humanity as they go.

Amoral psychopaths can best use such movements for their power-hungry orgies of destruction without having to be religious in the least. National Socialism in Germany was one of the more recent of these pseudo-religious delusions: Nazism's idea of the master people, the master race, was a delusion of grandeur, an identification with God! Stalin, too, deserves mention in this context. Stalinism was not primarily a nationalistic, but a pseudo-religious phenomenon, which is one reason many in Western European countries admired and idolized Stalin. He promised paradise on earth. To achieve his goal, Stalin sacrificed literally millions of people, while he was worshipped practically as a god. Today we grapple with all kinds of religious fundamentalists, Islamic, Hindu, Christians and others, all the product of this supra- or non-nationalistic phenomenon of religious mass movements.

Religion belongs to the human condition; religion is vital for the soul. At the same time, religion and its perversion, what I have called "pseudo-religion," continue to cause catastrophes and terrible wars. Should we, therefore, do away with religion? We might ask the same question in regard to nationalism. Just because aberrations could lead to atrocities does not necessarily mean that we have to oppose or do away with nationalism. The absence of national identification or, at the least, a weakness of such identification, has produced just as many if not more catastrophic consequences than the negative potential of nationalism. South America and Africa are examples of what I mean. There, military and commercial interests, family groupings and Mafia-like alliances assume power, move into existing vacuums. With egoistic groups like these, identification occurs on a more primitive, self-serving level and is not balanced by a greater national fantasy.

We might say that the Western Europe of today is in a fortunate position. To a large extent, it is composed of smoothly functioning nations gathered around relatively healthy national fantasies. These nations are no longer led by either imperialistic ideals and delusions or by religious perversions. We might, though, see a weakness of identity in the rapid change of the East German national fantasies. What about the European Community? Is it even capable of an identity? Only time will tell. Until now, the dominant fantasy of the European Community has been tied largely to questions of commerce and administration, a rather anemic fantasy, it seems to me. Can a purely commercial ideal symbolize humanity as a whole? I do not believe it will suffice to simply have an identity as "Europeans!" If so, the fantasy will have to include more than just freedom for business and commerce. It will have to include more than unlimited travel for freight trucks or cheap Sicilian oranges in Lapland and inexpensive reindeer meat in Sicily.

The common fantasy which the European Community has assumed is unbelievably dry, lean and even antiquated. In the preceding centuries the idea of oneness, of unification and of union, inspired many nations: Italy, Germany and others. The fantasy of unification, I fear, has in many respects lost its momentum. Fewer nations and fewer individuals today believe in all seriousness that miracles can happen through unification, through union. Interestingly enough, it is just this antiquated fantasy of unification that plays such a major role in the European Community. Strangely, the fantasy of the Community almost completely lacks the utopian element. Most national fantasies include utopian elements, if only the desire to be able to reach utopia. The deplorable spectacle of western intellectuals rejoicing over the mass murderers, Stalin and Mao Tse-Tung, might appear a little less *degoutant*, less disgusting, if we accept the naive longing for the possibility of utopia expressed in their adulation. Can as limited a fantasy as that of the European Community satisfy in the least this longing of ours?

We are living in an age of the secularization or, we might say, of the repression of the divine. Until now almost all national fantasies have also had a religious side. The Swiss Federal Constitution, for example, begins with the words, "In the name of God," while the British Queen is the head of the Anglican Church. Although nations like France and the United States are completely laicized, behind the national fantasies of these peoples stands a certain, almost religious belief in the potential of humankind: *"Liberte, Egalite, Fraternite,"* or "All men are created equal." As a minimum, most national fantasies include allusions to religion in so far as all religions are accepted and may be practiced. The European Community's fantasy in this regard is notably lacking, being neither religious nor devoutly anti-religious. Where are we to find the inspiring, the utopian, or even the religious elements in the Community's fantasies? Perhaps in the area of human rights? Yet, the EC's human rights' principles are not at all specific to Europe. They are more American than anything else. We must, therefore, assume that the current and felicitous national fantasies of the Western Europeans will not so quickly be supplemented or replaced by a truly viable fantasy common to the European Community.

Eastern Europe has had a harder time of it than the West. For years the Eastern Block countries attempted to create a supra-national Soviet individual. They based their attempt in part on the grandiose, pseudo-religious fantasy that we humans were capable of bringing about paradise on earth. Now, all of a sudden, the nations themselves are again popping to the surface from beneath the Soviet delusions: Latvia, Lithuania, Armenia, Estonia, Azerbaijan, Kazakhstan, Uzbekistan and the like. What are their fantasies as nations? The imperial notions of the Russian nation lived on into the era of the Soviets, but what effect will they continue to have for peoples of the smaller, onetime republics? Might not these smaller nations, impaired by decades of repression, have imperialistic fantasies of their own — pathologically compensatory ones at that? Might they not again succumb to pseudo-religious, supra-national delusions? As I write this — in the winter of 1992 — the peoples of the country we once knew as Yugoslavia are slaughtering one another. I do not take this as evidence against the possibility of a healthy nationalism as I understand it. It will take many decades for these peoples to recover from the uncertainty of centuries-long repression at the hands of Turks, Austrians and Germans, among others and to again establish new, cohesive fantasies.

We might well ask other questions regarding nationalism. How can national identity be possible at all given the great migration of people today? How, for example, will a woman find any identity if she were born of Turkish parents, she grew up in Germany, immigrated to Switzerland at sixteen and currently works for a Japanese company? What happens in cases of nationally mixed marriages, which will soon comprise a majority of marriages? Perhaps they are instances of a kind of national "no-man's land," a "no identity land?" Perhaps. A nation, as I have defined it above, is a group that gathers around a fantasy with general, human characteristics and which is open to everyone. The son of the extremely internationally minded English writer, Anthony Burgess, discovered suddenly at about the age of twenty that he belonged to the Scots. This fantasy persisted even though he had lived in Scotland very little and not a single drop of Scottish blood flowed in his veins. These days he wanders around Scotland in a kilt and gets terribly upset when unknowing foreigners confuse the Scots with the English or seem to believe that Edinburgh is an English city. I might also call to mind the Italian who proudly showed me the results of his factory's production and said, "That is true Swiss quality!"

We could also consider the question of multiple national identifications. An increasing number of individuals and families identify with more than one national fantasy. I remember a flight to Rome one time on which the majority of the passengers were young Swiss, who loudly and freely spoke Swiss German to each other. As we approached our landing in Rome, I was suddenly surrounded by Italians: the speech, mannerisms and gestures of the young people had become typically Italian. What were they, Swiss or Italians? As I discovered, they were descendants of Italian immigrants to Switzerland and identified, therefore, with two different national fantasies.

Of course, conflicts of loyalty can easily arise with this kind of double, even triple national identity, but multiple identity can also lead to a greater sensitivity and an unusual level of awareness. It is probably no coincidence that the Jews, who for hundreds or thousands of years have had to maintain a double identity, have produced so many outstanding psychologists. Many of us humans live in a complicated web of identifications, general and national on the one hand, specific and cultural on the other.

The theme of collective identification that I have dealt with here through the phenomenon of the Nation, is endlessly complicated. Our social, economic and cultural situations change constantly. Our collective identification assumes other forms, expresses itself differently. What happens to the old identification fantasies and their adherents? Will the Indians in England or the Tamils in Switzerland identify with the local patterns of life? Will an altogether new identity evolve? I think of the Sikh I once saw in Glasgow with a turban fashioned from material with a Scots' tartan pattern. I think, too, of the response of a black man in Edinburgh who, when asked what he felt his identity to be, answered proudly, "I am a black Scotsman!" Will almost all of us identify with multiple national fantasies in the future or just the fantasy of our nation of origin? To what extent will individuals experience extensive identity conflicts?

Nationalism and nations promise a bright future if we humans can understand the Nation as a community of fantasy, loved easily and playfully but passionately. Can we see the Nation as being without any claims to domination, not cramped, not fanatical, accessible to all, representative of a special kind of humanity. Fundamentally, the Nation has nothing to do with genetics, offering rather to all a specific configuration for the human condition. Because of our individual origins, personal development and basic life decisions, a particular nation, a given fantasy, appeals to some of us more than others. This phenomenon promises a peaceful, colorful world filled with interesting, individual and collective possibilities for identifying with humanity. With Gottfried Keller we might well say, "Treasure every man's fatherland, but love your own."

CHAPTER 7

NO ANSWER TO JOB

"Arteriosclerosis is the result of a particular mind set; Gastric ulcers are the cost of swallowing anger and rage." Comment of a participant in a colloquium on psychosomatic disorders, *1983*

This and the following chapters carry the paradoxical approach to psychology even a step further than the preceding ones. I will first address a tragic paradox, one of suffering, and then, in the final chapter, the playful paradox of unknowing — Socrates' "I know that I do not know."

Our capacity to enjoy life and to thoroughly exhaust all of our potential depends to a large extent on a healthy and properly functioning body. When disease strikes us our potential and our ability to live according to that potential is severely diminished. Disease, like other kinds of misfortune, calls out for explanation and justification. Ethnologists tell us that the so-called archaic cultures often linked disease with witchcraft and magic. Accordingly, an evil spirit or person stands behind every malaise. Until only recently, we in Europe believed that witches were capable of causing disease. Jews were blamed for the plague during the Middle Ages, being accused of poisoning the drinking water. We often believe that God, Himself, punishes the sinner with disease in much the same way as He punished humanity with floods, fire storms and earthquakes.

Our tendency to disparage those who are unfortunate and sick also has its roots in the Bible. The Bible describes Job, for example, as a god-fearing, pious and highly respectable man. Misfortune overtook him. He lost all of his goods and became severely ill. The friends who visited him accused him of grievous sins and explained to him that he needed to see his misfortune as God's punishment. As moderns, of course, we have certainly left such a conception of disease behind us — or have we?

The classical, orthodox medicine of the 19th and 20th Centuries has attempted to understand disease "scientifically." It has not taken religion, morality and to some extent, psychology into account. Instead medicine understands the human body as a complicated machine, as a highly specialized chemical factory. This unbelievably complicated mechanism can be disturbed or damaged for a great variety of reasons. It has been the task of medicine to find the mechanical, chemical and other reasons for the malfunction and to correct them. This purely technical, scientific understanding of the human body has enabled medicine to make impressive progress in fighting disease.

At the beginning of the 20th century, psychology began to make its voice heard. Many physicians were no longer satisfied with the mechanistic and chemical approach to disease, attempting instead to conceive and understand physical disease by way of the psyche. Psychosomatic medicine began to develop as a discipline and it suggested the presence of psychological disturbances behind the facade of many diseases. Certain diseases are quite clearly psychosomatic in nature, a fact supported by experiments with animals and humans. Rage and frustration, for example, alter the chemical balance in the stomach and cause ulcers. An excess of what we call "stress" leads to elevated blood pressure. We cannot deny that a connection exists between certain psychological conditions and physical disorders. These experimentally demonstrated connections, though, have unleashed a flood of psychosomatic fantasies. Many believe that unexplained diseases such as cancer can be understood psychologically. Numerous physicians and psychologists use this approach for the majority of diseases. They maintain that Arteriosclerosis, the narrowing of the blood vessels, is due to an unduly narrow perspective or attitude. They would see breast cancer as a negative relationship to one's femininity.

If we examine the explanation and meaning psychosomatic medicine gives to disease more closely, we make a curious discovery. Psychosomatic medicine considers every disease a kind of punishment for a particular sin, namely the sin of imbalanced psychological development. We never hear that someone became physically ill because he or she was extremely balanced psychologically or was capable of expressing feelings or was demonstrably caring. Instead psychosomatic medicine attempts to continually prove that unsuccessful psychological development almost automatically leads to physical diseases.

It is certainly tempting to view the body, with its functions and dysfunctions, as the symbolic expression of psychological life, as the language of the soul. We need to remember that this perspective deals primarily with fantasies. The fantastical nature of psychosomatic explanations of diseases manifests in the fact that such explanations can seldom be proved experimentally or scientifically. Most psychosomatic theories find their "proof" in anecdotes. Psychological typologies of individuals who suffer from different disorders come and go. We hear the fantasy that executives tend to have high blood pressure and then we hear that junior executives are especially prone to high blood pressure since they have not managed to become executives. We hear that excessive ambition lies behind many psychosomatic conditions, but then we have to ask ourselves why many Finnish lumberjacks suffer high blood pressure. Are they, then, overly ambitious?

What disturbs me about the fantasy quality of psychosomatic medicine is its moralism. All of these marvelously symbolical, modern explanations of disease are, due to their moralism, extremely harmful. People who are sick not only have to suffer from their diseases, but must also feel guilty in addition. This includes individuals who suffer from cancer, or those who are destroyed by horrible infections, or those who deteriorate due to chronic diseases like arteriosclerosis. Their disease is their sole misdoing. They failed to develop properly psychologically or they repressed their feelings or they did not repress their feelings enough or they were overly giving or they were not giving enough. This psychosomatic moralism harms in many ways, in many forms. Not only does it create sinners, but Pharisees as well and the Pharisees despise the sinners! I often overhear my colleagues talking condescendingly about their patients with psychosomatic diseases.

Before I continue, I would like to add a comment to avoid any misunderstanding. I feel we have to clearly differentiate between morality and a moralistic attitude or moralism. Moralism is a perversion or caricature of morality. We can never be moral enough! Morality is the attempt to follow the lead of Eros, to abide by guidelines that make it possible for us to do more good than evil. Moralism or being moralistic, on the other hand, misuses these guidelines. The Pharisee, for example, is moralistic and uses the rules of morality to denigrate his fellow man.

Would it not be better in our relations with disease to become somewhat more "agnostic," to admit our unknowing? We have no idea what this life is all about, but above all we have no idea what disease is all about. Collectively and individually we can easily tolerate this lack of knowledge about the meaning of life and the meaning of disease as long as things are going well. When catastrophe overtakes us as disease, then our lack of knowledge becomes almost unbearable. This was certainly the case for the Old Testament figure, Job. In my opinion, the Bible is one of the greatest psychological and religious works of all time. Old Testament scholars believe that the beginning and the conclusion of the Book of Job were a later addition. They maintain that the actual story is that of the pious, moral and God-fearing man called Job who was beset with disease and misfortune. His friends assumed that he was a sinner, punished by God for his misdeeds. For his part, Job rejected their accusations. He could simply not understand why he had to suffer so, why God had sent him so much misery.

When God finally spoke to him, he offered Job no real explanation. He announced simply that He, God, had created everything and that He ruled over everything.

The beginning of the story narrates God's bet with Satan. God bets that Satan will not be able to cause God's true servant, Job, to doubt. As I mentioned, this introduction was probably added at a later date. This addition dilutes the awfulness of the story by attempting to represent the events with more meaning and by softening what is most objectionable. The core of the story is Job's suffering and God's response to that suffering. God's answer, however, was no answer at all. He offered no explanation for Job's horrendous suffering. The Book of Job is remarkable because it looks catastrophe, misery, disease and suffering in the eye. It does not evade the issues through some kind of explanation, particularly not a moralistic one. The story simply relates how God torments human beings and gives no explanation.

I am of the opinion that it would be better to regard disease above all as a tragedy, as a horrible occurrence without meaning and content. This does not mean that we should not use disease when it does strike us. An ambitious junior executive who works day and night does not fall ill with hepatitis because he has to be forced to take life a little easier. Seen psychologically, his ambition is not particularly sinful. Once he *is* sick and has to take everything a little slower, he can use his increased time off to reflect on himself and his way of life. The fact that we can use disease to our advantage does not at all mean that we became sick because we were psychological sinners! Disease not only gives us much when we know how to make the best out of the circumstances. Disease also has something to give us when we can see it as a tragedy, as an inexplicable act of God or of Nature. We Jungians regard one's individuation process, his search for wholeness, as being just as important as his search for health and well-being. Individuation is not only the striving to become conscious, but also the experience of coming in contact with the Self, with the divine spark in each of us.

Could it not be that confrontation with the apparent meaninglessness of catastrophes might further the transcendental aspect of Individuation? Might we not further individuation by understanding our diseases as tragedy as Job did or by our accepting misery and physical suffering as incomprehensible acts of God? If we could take these positions we would individuate in the sense of actually coming in contact with "our" divine spark. This was Job's experience when he understood his misery and suffering to be incomprehensible and not the result of specific sins. Job's reward for his courageous confrontation with the incomprehensibility of suffering was that God spoke to him. God did not, of course, explain anything, but he *did* reveal Himself. What more could a human being desire? How many of us can say of ourselves that we personally spoke with God? If the acceptance of the tragic incomprehensibility of disease had as its result God speaking to us, then our terrible experience would have been worthwhile.

I do not wish to completely reject the aesthetic and wonderfully beautiful symbolism of psychosomatic mythologies and fantasies. While they are thoroughly stimulating, they have limited significance. All psychosomatic theories, fantasies and mythologies are moving expressions of a profound belief in life. Although we cannot understand disease, suffering and catastrophe, we can believe in a religious sense that some kind of meaning hides in all the ghastly things which we have to experience. Thus we find differentiated, aesthetic explanations for all the misery we suffer, and we express these explanations so symbolically that we believe our suffering actually does have a meaning. We have to understand psychosomatic theories as legends, pointing to the transcendental side of our disease and our misery. Psychosomatic fantasies only become absurd when we take them as scientific explanations and not as mythology.

We can confront disease as Gnostics or as agnostics, as knowing or as unknowing. Both kinds of *Auseinandersetzung* have their advantages and disadvantages. Psychosomatic medicine of today tends to be Gnostic, tends to know the meaning of disease or at least the symbolic meaning. A powerful psychosomatic mythology has evolved in the last few years which often rests on minimal connections to scientific medicine. Frequently, this mythology is nothing but pure poetry, which, as I have already mentioned, definitely serves a purpose. At the same time, we ought not to forget that the agnostic perspective of psychosomatic medicine is also important and valuable. The agnostic perspective offers no legends, but looks the inexplicable tragedy of disease in the face as Job did. Who knows? Perhaps like Job, we will develop further psychologically through God's not answering us, but speaking to us nevertheless.

We can compare the Gnostic and agnostic perspectives of psychosomatic medicine with the two opposing positions with which Christians and the followers of other religions attempted to understand God. Some prayed in the desert surrounded by sand and stones; others filled their churches with beautiful images and statues which represented God in all His glory. We cannot deny that the body often has something to tell us, even though it may be difficult to understand. Does the body really intend to tell us a moralistic story? It seems to me that frequently unpleasant and fully unconscious individuals enjoy surprisingly good health into advanced old age, while on the other hand, friendly and highly conscious individuals suffer from the most horrible diseases. Could it be that malevolence and unconsciousness are, in themselves, healthier?

Is it not high time that psychosomatic medicine dispensed with its moralism? Moralism is the most simplistic and childish way of understanding what happens to us as human beings. Good people are rewarded and bad people are punished. This is the message of hundreds of cowboy movies and detective stories. In spite of its simplistic nature, this mythology that "the good are rewarded and the bad punished" is not entirely false. It underlines in a moving and naive way the importance of morality. It is terribly important for us as human beings to be moral. Life without morality (not moralism!) would literally be hell. Where the law of the jungle rules, there is little happiness and any psychological development becomes much more difficult.

Moralistic psychosomatic mythologies have their uses, if somewhat limited. With simple stories they emphasize the importance of morality. Are the disadvantages, though, not greater than the advantages? They strengthen our feelings of guilt which are at the root of much of our psychological suffering. We can, therefore, hope that our colleagues in psychosomatic medicine will continue to spin legends and fantastical stories against the backdrop of physical diseases. We need to listen carefully to them to hear what the body wants to tell us, remembering that its language, unfortunately, is often incomprehensible.

CHAPTER 8

THE BASILISK — AUTONOMOUS SEXUALITY

"Sexuality is something very natural." A sex-education pamphlet, 1986

We Jungians generally attempt to describe psychological phenomena with images instead of with concepts. In this chapter, therefore, I will explore the phenomenon of sexuality through the image of the basilisk, a mythological animal of the Middle Ages, which was said to represent sexual desire.

The name basilisk comes from the Greek word basiliscos, meaning "little king" or "cock with the golden comb," and is mentioned for the first time in Psalm 91, verse 13. In the Vulgate translation, this verse reads, "*Super aspidem et basiliscum ambulabis. . . ,*" "thou wilt walk over the asp and the basilisk."[1] The basilisk is a most peculiar and fascinating animal. It has the body of a snake, a pointed head and a three-part comb. It was born out of an egg (which had no yolk) laid by a cock and hatched by a toad upon a dung heap. Furthermore, the animal has a three-part tail, glittering eyes and a crown on its head. Its gaze, some say even its breath, can kill an attacker. One could only approach it in the same manner in which one approached the Gorgon

---

[1] Compare the King James version: "Thou shalt tread upon the lion and the adder. .

Medusa, with a mirror. The only animal that was a match for this fabled creature was the weasel. The weasel would spring forward, fall back, attack here and attack there as the occasion presented itself. It fought pragmatically.

The Latin of the Middle Ages used the word *luxuria* for lust. Lust was represented as a being, riding upon a wild sow, wearing a wreath of roses and holding a shield before it. On this shield was the supposed basilisk. Generally, though, the basilisk was a symbol for lust, lasciviousness and *luxuria*. It was dangerous, fascinating and difficult to comprehend or to categorize zoologically. The basilisk seems to me to be the best representation of lustful sexuality that I have ever encountered.

I would like to offer some examples of the activity of this peculiar creature. A couple has been married for thirty years — he is fifty-eight and she is fifty-three — and continues to lead a satisfying sexual life with constant variety. Or a thirty-five year old senior executive experiences a purely sexual, Dionysian adventure with a ship's officer during a Mediterranean cruise. Or a mother and grandmother who lives for her family steals away periodically for a weekend of passionate love-making with her lover of twenty years. Such experiences are the felicitous effects of the basilisk. We often find the other side of the basilisk's activities on the front pages of tabloids. A recent situation in the United States provides a ready illustration.

There was a vacancy on the American Supreme Court which President Bush needed to fill. This court has extremely broad authority. Not only does it make rulings on purely legal questions, but it also rules on the constitutionality of any law which has been passed. In some ways, it is the political conscience of the United States. President Bush appointed Clarence Thomas, a black man, to fill the vacant position. Since most Americans considered him to be unqualified, he was controversial and there were many who opposed his confirmation. Near the end of the confirmation hearings, Anita Hill, a thirty-four year old woman, a University of Oklahoma law professor and also black, appeared with some unfavorable testimony about Thomas. To be sure, she emphasized that she had not wanted to discuss this subject in public but had been asked to do so. She related that ten years earlier, while he had been her superior, Clarence Thomas had harassed her with obscene comments, off-color jokes and sexual allusions that were embarrassing for her. He had, for example, referred to a pornographic movie titled "Long Dong Silver," whose main character was a black man with an unusually large sexual organ. He had also discussed group sex and similar matters in front of her, she claimed. Her testimony made the confirmation of this man seem almost impossible. Thomas, himself, denied ever having made such sexual allusions in the presence of the professor, then a bureaucrat. She remained by her testimony.

The story is noteworthy regardless of what is true and what is not. Should it develop that Clarence Thomas did harass Anita Hill with sexual remarks ten years ago, it would be very peculiar. To become a justice of the Supreme Court of the United States is extremely difficult since this is a much sought after office. It is a lifetime position. Justices are highly regarded and have a good income, not to mention social prestige. For these reasons, we have to assume that Clarence Thomas is quite ambitious and probably always has been. Ten years ago he would have been just as ambitious, doing whatever was necessary to further his career. That such an intelligent and ambitious man would have endangered this career just to satisfy his appetite for sexual humor seems truly unusual. That such a dedicated and intelligent man could be so driven by sexuality to the point of risking his life's ambition, proves at least that this basilisk is also capable of much destruction.

The uncanny effects of the basilisk's activities manifest themselves repeatedly. A major problem in Zürich and probably in many parts of Europe, is the so-called "condom-hating" males, (men who seek out prostitutes for sexual intercourse without using condoms). Usually professional prostitutes are unwilling to expose themselves to the obvious risks. These males, therefore, turn to girls who are drug addicts, who have to have money to feed their habits and who prostitute themselves without being able to say "No" to anything. It is not difficult to imagine the kind of risks these men incur for themselves, their families and their community at large. Many of the addicted girls are HIV positive; most of the men are married. For the sake of a momentary sexual titillation, they risk the lives and health of themselves, their wives and their children.

The confrontation with sexuality and the attempt to control the basilisk is probably as old as humanity. Certainly since the beginning of recorded time, mankind has tried to tame this strange animal, at least in the Christianized part of the western world. From the beginning, Christianity took up the struggle against the basilisk most energetically. One of the Church's methods of combating this animal has been to represent it as the greatest of evils. Lust or lasciviousness is one of the seven deadly sins: *superbia* (pride), *invidia* (envy), *ira* (anger), *tristitia* (sadness), *avaritia* (avarice), *gula* (greed) and , finally, *luxuria* (lust or lasciviousness). One of the Church fathers, Hugo St. Victor, placed luxuria first on the list of the deadly sins. If someone died without having repented a deadly sin, he did not receive absolution and went to hell for all eternity. In this kind of confrontation, the Church has sought to dominate the basilisk primarily by emphasizing its sinister aspects.

The Church has attempted furthermore to get a hold on the basilisk, *luxuria*, through the institution of marriage. In the Middle Ages, all sexual intercourse outside of marriage was forbidden, at least officially. That was not all. Even within marriage, sexual relations between husband and wife were not permitted on Sundays or on official church holy days. Practically speaking, this meant that the church forbade sexual activity on one hundred and sixty days of the year. These limitations were very harsh and were probably not observed except by Saints.

We have a tendency to lay the blame for the sexual miseries of the last several centuries, for the radical struggle against the basilisk, on the Reformers. Not only did they frequently establish extremely strict rules regarding sexual behavior, but they actually followed these rules and attempted to enforce them. This perspective, of course, is not completely accurate. Ulrich Zwingli of Zürich, next to Calvin, one of the most significant Reformers, and Luther, one of the strict fathers of the Reformation, was once attacked for his wild sexual life as a young man. He wrote, "It is naturally true that I have slept with many women, but I have never laid hands on a virgin and I have never crawled into the bed of a married woman." The Council of Zürich which named him to be the pastor of the Grossmuenster[2] questioned him about the fact that he had apparently sired an illegitimate child while he was pastor in Einsiedeln. Zwingli supposedly replied, "But she was so incredibly beautiful."

During the time of Queen Victoria, the basilisk was apparently locked up and restricted as seldom before in the history of Europe. The intention of taking this horrifying beast into custody did not work exactly as planned. The sexual life of the Victorians was decidedly vital and lively. It was the high tide of bordellos, pornography, of secret and not-so-secret extramarital affairs, all of which flourished side by side with the official Victorian morality.

The battle or the striving to contain, to lock up, the basilisk is never ending. Catholic theologians even today seek to tame the beast by affirming sexuality, but only within marriage and then only when it serves procreation. Birth control, therefore, is not allowed. Sexuality is naturally linked with procreation, but not as much as we might think. I would say that ninety-nine percent of sexual life has nothing at all to do with procreation. I understand sexuality, of course, in a broader sense, as including not just sexual intercourse, but all sexual fantasies, dreams, masturbation and so forth. If we were to trace the life of the average mortal from the cradle to the grave, we would ascertain that the greatest percentage of sexual life occurs in dreams and fantasies which have little to do with procreation. We seldom engage in sexual activity, per se, to produce children. Perhaps we might see sexuality among animals as serving the instinctual perpetuation of the species, but even that seems questionable. There are so many marvelous, fantastic and unique courtship rituals — think of the peacock's spreading its tail — that we might ask ourselves if these elaborate demonstrations only serve to increase the population.

Protestant theologians, among others, are representative of yet another approach in the attempt to subdue and domesticate the basilisk. They admit without hesitation that sexuality and

[2] The church which would be the "cathedral" of Zürich if the Swiss Reformed Church used this term..

procreation do not necessarily have anything to do with each other. At the same time, they stress that sexuality should be regarded as a function of human relationship. In this they find support from psychologists. They teach and preach sexuality as something wonderful as long as it is understood as the expression of relationship between men and women. As long as sexuality is the expression of the love for one's (heterosexual) partner, it is beautiful and morally acceptable. We hear, however, that pure, free, what some might call wanton sexuality, *luxuria*, the basilisk, is a tragic thing. It must be rejected. At best we can experience it as typical of human bestiality, as the expression of an immature, animal-like nature.

To regard sexuality solely as a function of relationship seems much too narrow to me. The reality of the situation is totally different. A major portion of sexual life — consisting not only of sexual activity, but of sexual dreams and fantasies — has very little to do with relationship. Most sexual fantasies have to do with vague, unknown partners or with those with whom an actual relationship would be catastrophic. Within a marriage, sexuality can often be very fruitful and can promote relationship. It can just as often, however, destroy a marriage.

The disciples of relationship receive unexpected reinforcement from the feminists, who accuse men of treating women as sexual objects. The feminists protest that men live out their sexuality with women without any kind of feeling or relationship. Is it not true that just as many women use or abuse men as sexual objects as the other way around, at least in fantasy? These days the problem of sexual molestation — and here I do not mean the violent kind, but the kind I have described in the case of Judge Thomas — is very much in our awareness. Women justifiably assert themselves against it. I feel that the battle is heading in the wrong direction. We should not place the emphasis so much on men's harassment, verbal and otherwise, of women. It is more a question of women's ability to harass men, of emerging from the passive roles superimposed on them by our culture. The Swiss feminist, Iris von Roten, proposed this kind of change thirty years ago in her book, *Women in the Playpen (Frauen im Laufgitter)*.

Freud attempted to accomplish the integration or the conquering of the basilisk with an admirable yet grandiose radicalism. For him, sexuality is *the* energy, *the* libido, which moves and drives us humans as living beings. Freud considered everything that humanity dreams or wishes, everything that we create, an expression of direct or sublimated sexuality. Sexuality is the origin of all human behavior, a demonic and basic instinct which constantly threatens to overrun the ego or the superego. To survive, the ego and superego must constantly erect barriers against the force of the basilisk, one reason why our attempts to contain sexuality are always destined to fail. Fortunately, we cannot so easily extinguish the source of all of our psychic energy. While Freud's perspective is radical and freeing, it is not phenomenologically convincing. At the risk of being simplistic, I will use an old argument. I have difficulty grasping how a painting by Titian or Picasso is but an expression of the anal erotic or how anyone could see such work as a sublimated wish to smear feces on the wall. Nor is it easy to reduce one of Bach's fugues to a form of the sexual drive. Freud, himself, admitted that although art reflects the soul of the artist, we cannot ultimately state or comprehend what determines art.

Jung examined and rejected these radical theories of Freud's and, in a manner of speaking, turned the whole question on its head. He maintained the theory that there is a general, psychological energy which can flow in different channels. One of those channels is sexuality. From this perspective, sexuality or the activity of the basilisk is but a part. It occupies only one of the channels of psychic energy in general. For Jung, the remarkable and manifold sexual activities, dreams and fantasies are nothing other than intensively experienced symbols of the overall psychological development of individuals, of self discovery and among others, of individuation.

One of the greatest challenges of psychological development is the confrontation with and the unification of psychic opposites. These opposites assume many forms in our experience and expression of them: conscious and unconscious, good and evil, living and dead and, last but not least, female and male, woman and man. We experience the *mysterium coniunctionis,* as the alchemists called it, the secret of union (of the opposites) most intensively in physical sexuality, in the way in which human beings encounter each other sexually in activity, fantasy and dream. Such experience does not necessarily happen in the context of a feeling relationship but often occurs within free, autonomous sexuality. It occurs through the purely physical/sexual or through the fantasized encounter with other individuals, men and women. Sexuality is the living, experiencing of the symbol of the *mysterium coniunctionis.* The love songs the nuns sang to Christ in Switzerland's Tosstal do not necessarily have to be understood as sublimated sexuality. On the contrary, physically experienced sexuality is a living, effective symbol of the existential confrontation of the opposites.

Even (or especially?) our relationship with God expresses itself through sexual images or is suggested in the physical/ sexual. The love poems of the Persian poet, Hafiz, are not a symptom of the sexual frustration of an aging man but the expression of the mystical experience within sexuality, the encounter with God. The same holds true for Solomon's *Song of Songs* and the novels of Henry Miller. It holds true for the popular hit songs with their repetitive, "I love you, I love you." The latter do not primarily express the biological sexual longing of youth, but rather youth's longing for psychological development, for individuation, for the union of opposites. The millions of love songs are actually songs about individuation, about psyche's development and about relationship with God.

Jung stressed that one of the most important tasks of psychological maturity is the confrontation with the shadow, with the destructive, with the murderer and self-murderer in us. Masochism and sadism are therefore, from Jung's perspective, an experience of our shadow through the medium of sexuality. Masochism, this completely unnatural sexual desire for suffering pain, expresses the Auseinandersetzung, even the acceptance of a suffering which is so destructive for us. This destructive suffering reaches its zenith in our self-murderous tendencies. We can see sadism as the murderer and destroyer in us expressed through the medium of sexuality. Sadistic and masochistic sexuality, lived out or fantasized — the fantasies are quite widespread, while the concrete activities are somewhat less frequent—are living symbols of individuation.

Even the wonderful attempt on the part of Jungian psychology to understand sexuality—including purely physical, autonomous sexuality—as symbolic of psychological development is not completely satisfying and leaves many questions open. The basilisk rears its head anew as an autonomous force, as a *daimon*, which cannot be tamed. The obsessive monotony of many sexual fantasies and of the greater part of sexual life in general can not be seen as only individuation symbolism. Too, sexuality is frequently so destructive, so far removed from the soul, that it seems forced to consider it symbolically. The basilisk gives us no peace. Its power is so great that it terrorizes us even in its absence. Let me explain what I mean.

Many contemporary psychologists, particularly those influenced by Freud's psychology, regard asexuality or extremely weak or mild sexuality as the result of neurotic development. I would guess that approximately one fifth of the human race has a very limited interest in sexuality. It has little importance for them and they do not consider it a crucial part of life. They may occasionally participate in sexual activity. They may want to have children and use sexuality for that reason. They are not, however, truly gripped by sexuality. These basically asexual individuals are not taken seriously by contemporary psychology. At best, psychology may murmur something about repression or the like.

There are individuals who, for example, have absolutely no musical talent nor any need for music whatsoever. Dr. Samuel Johnson once said, "Music is one of the noises which disturbs me least." There are many individuals whose relationship to sexuality is much the same. As a rule we leave these nonmusical types alone and do not accuse them of being neurotic. (There are, of course, music pedagogues who maintain that there is no such thing as a nonmusical human being. Their perspective, though, does not correspond with the facts of the matter.) There are always those to whom music means nothing and who have no musical ability at all. In the same way, there are those for whom sexuality is unimportant. This minority has a difficult time of it: in modern psychology asexuality does not exist except as a neurotic manifestation or as a form of extreme inhibition.

The power of the basilisk makes itself known through this lack of recognition for those who are asexual. The basilisk must be found in everyone. We have, thank God, given up trying to change homosexuals into heterosexuals. We have not yet given up trying to change asexual human beings into sexual ones. If a young man or a young woman at twenty-five shows little interest in sexuality and has perhaps never engaged in sexual intercourse, the psychologist wrinkles his brow. The psychiatrist assumes the presence of a severe psychological disturbance, some early childhood trauma, a negative mother or some incestuous experience. The patient in question believes in the same way that he or she is severely disturbed psychologically. If need be, psychologists and psychiatrists can accept sexual perversions of the strangest sort. Asexuality, though, may not be tolerated. The Roman Catholic Church is more tolerant. It knows the images of St. Joseph's marriage, the asexual marriage and of celibacy as possible forms of sexual expression. The drawback in the Roman Church's attitude is that it automatically assumes that asexuality is the same as a vocation to the priesthood.

There are and have been other attempts to deal with the basilisk, primarily to contain it, to completely extinguish it or to minimize it. After the First World War, for example, it was fashionable to equate sexuality with quenching one's thirst, with taking a drink of water, as if it were a harmless, biological need. Regardless of the approach we take, we always run into limitations. Neither the attempt to contain sexuality by relating it to procreation and marriage, nor the conceptualizing of sexuality as a function of relationship have succeeded in neutralizing the power of the basilisk. The same holds true for Freud's radical proposal of sexuality as the root of life as well as for Jung's aesthetic, elegant and fundamental suggestion that sexuality be seen as symbolic of individuation. None of these perspectives have been truly successful, no matter how interesting and inspiring. Apparently, we can never master nor domesticate the basilisk.

I am beginning to ask myself if the time has not come to

cease our efforts to completely control and to tame the basilisk? Should we not concede that it continues to be incomprehensible, unclassifiable and ungraspable? We would then have no normalizing of sexuality, no "normal" or "abnormal" sexuality and no sexual morality. We would have but one, generalized moral standard which would also apply to sexuality: *We should not harm other human beings and, if possible, not harm ourselves as well; we should love others, or at least behave as we would if we did love them.* There would be no specifically "moral" sexuality nor would there be such a thing as sexual normality.

Would it not be better and more realistic, more effective from a therapeutic, pedagogic or social view point to recognize our inability to contain sexuality? The human psyche includes many forces which we cannot integrate and which by far exceed our comprehension. In the last hundred years, the heroic ego has sought to become the dictator of the psyche. This fact finds expression in modern psychology when we speak of "ego psychology" or of a strong and a weak ego, or when we describe how, in psychotherapy, the ego must be strengthened. From this heroic standpoint, it is painful to be forced to acknowledge that sexuality has successfully resisted all attempts to defeat it, to bring it under the control of the ego. It is difficult to accept that all efforts to "integrate" sexuality and to unite its voice in the general harmony of the psyche have failed. Is it not time to simply respect the fact that we cannot control sexuality, that we cannot integrate it and that we cannot completely understand it? At best we can describe it phenomenologically. Sexuality is here, it is there, sometimes weak and sometimes strong, now in this form, now in that. Some of us have a strong drive toward autonomous sexuality. Some can shape and form their relationships through sexuality while for others, sexuality undermines and destroys relationships.

Sexuality can assault us when we least expect it. It can harass us and delight us. It is beautiful and ugly, demonic and divine. It may even be absent. It is just like the basilisk. Would it not be better to simply stop all this moralizing, pathologizing, integrating and normalizing? Does not legend tell us that the weasel is the only animal which can deal with the basilisk? The weasel does not confront but relates to the basilisk pragmatically, approaching here and there and retreating when retreat is appropriate. The weasel avoids the basic struggle and never thinks about taming the basilisk. It would be senseless for the weasel to place moral or normative demands on the basilisk. Given the weasel's example we can ask ourselves what would give us a pragmatic, non-moralizing, non-normalizing relationship with sexuality? I feel that an agnostic, pragmatic attitude would be very much to our benefit. We expend a tremendous amount of energy in trying to dominate or integrate sexuality, in trying to come to terms with it morally, to understand it psychologically and to use it socially.

All the forms we have discussed of relating to sexuality lead in the end to torment, guilt feelings and the experience of failure (unless we can remain light and playful at the same time). This is true whether we are talking about the moralizing of sexuality or the utilitarian attempt to grasp sexuality by restricting it to procreation. This is the case whether we identify with the romantic approach of seeing sexuality as a function of relationship or with the subjugation of sexuality to the ego and the superego. This is also true of the Jungian treatment of sexuality as symbolic. We already feel like failures or fairly neurotic or somewhat unclean, like moral weaklings . Even the "Marcusian" (from the neomarxist theorist, Herbert Marcuse) delusion is of no help. Marcuse held the superstition that we will all be able to joyfully give in to sexuality when we have done away with our repressive society. Evil capitalism is not what hinders our living out and enjoying sexuality but the autonomy of sexuality, itself, is. In its autonomy, sexuality has little consideration for our lives, our needs or the needs of our fellow human beings. Sexuality can be useful. It can also be extremely harmful and destructive.

By recognizing the autonomy of sexuality, by recognizing the strength, the uniqueness and the stubbornness of the basilisk, we could prevent innumerable complications. We could avoid much of what makes us neurotic by accepting the puzzling sovereignty of sexuality and by respecting its differing manifestations without fanatical claims to understanding or control. We could do the basilisk the honor of recognizing its powerful and demonic aspects while at the same time observing it closely and protecting ourselves when necessary. In this regard, we have made some progress in the last few years. We no longer tyrannize homosexuals as much. We accept masturbation (an impressive manifestation of the basilisk, incidentally, now compulsive/terrifying, now relaxing/exciting) to some extent, more than in the past.

Many people believe that sexuality shows consideration for the psyche as a whole, a belief that confuses the power of sexual attraction with a soul connection. True, the two often appear together, and this is very delightful. Many marriages, though, came into being because autonomous sexuality appeared and was mistaken for love. Often marriages are built on this misunderstood foundation. Thousands of marriages which owe their origin to the basilisk founder especially when this autonomous sexuality suddenly turns its focus on someone other than the husband or wife. It is particularly difficult for modern man to accept that there are completely independent forces at work in his psyche. In earlier times people spoke of demons, of possession, of being "beside oneself." While we today find these expressions curiously archaic, they are not completely unrealistic.

This brings us to a further use for a pragmatic capitulation to the basilisk. In psychology, it is of determining significance to constantly attempt to grasp and to understand the psychological phenomena, in this case sexuality. It is just as important to continually realize that all of our attempts are more than inadequate. Like the basilisk, the psyche never allows itself ultimately to be captured and understood. With Socrates we need to be able to say, "I know, that I know nothing."

It would be wrong to succumb to complete agnosticism, to throw up our hands and say, "I give up! I will never understand so let's just stop psychologizing!" We should never stop trying with the greatest of care to capture and understand the basilisk. Yet it escapes us time and again, just as the psyche continues to escape us and remains in the final analysis inexplicable and incomprehensible. Nowhere is our comprehension and lack of comprehension of the human psyche so obvious as in our explanations of sexuality and the basilisk. Nowhere else do we so clearly experience the Creator's confusing play and nowhere else is His play so exciting, so frustrating and so stimulating. Many of us are simply gripped by sexuality, for it is difficult to avoid.

Those of us who are religious should be joyful over our incomprehension of the basilisk. The basilisk shows us over and over that we cannot ultimately conceive of the miracle of human existence and that, to approach the human soul, we need other categories such as faith. Recognizing the inconceivability of the basilisk would help us to be better psychologists. It is not just the depths of the basilisk that we will never plumb, but those of the entire psyche as well. These are depths at which we can only hint with images, stories and mythologies. Psychological theories are not physical theories. Psychological theories are but explanatory models, are only attempts to approach the soul through stories and symbols.

In this sense, the image, the story of the basilisk is vastly superior to the biological attempts to provide explanations of sexuality: the basilisk must also be feared. It is never harmless, despite all attempts to the contrary to represent it as something harmlessly natural. The Christian theologians whom sexuality so intimidated were no fools. They were better psychologists than our modern-day, well-meaning educators who maintain that we can solve all our sexual problems by including sex education classes in our school curricula. The basilisk cannot be tamed. It is dangerous: its breath alone can kill. The basilisk is one reason why notions of open marriages as well as those of free, natural and unencumbered sexuality are extremely questionable. We should go ahead and play with the basilisk, but with the greatest of caution. It offers us what is most beautiful, most wonderful but also most dangerous.

The image of the basilisk gives me two possible ways to end this last chapter. The first possibility is religious. We can see the basilisk, which wears a crown on its head and is said to have a three-part tail and a three-part comb, as a shadow image of the Trinity, of God the Father, God the Son and God the Holy

Spirit. Autonomous sexuality, therefore, carries religious meaning and significance. As I discussed earlier, sexual experience and religion are closely linked to one another. An encounter with God, to paraphrase what I said in Chapter 5, can only occur when we experience the shadow side of God. We can experience God just as fully through the autonomy of the basilisk as we can through a breathtaking sunset. The basilisk, too, is an expression of God's love.

The second possibility for ending this chapter is agnostic. The Middle Ages designated autonomous sexuality, *luxuria* and symbolized it using the image of the basilisk. If we apply a somewhat dubious etymological trick, we have the progression, *luxuria, luxus* and *ludo* ("lust," "luxury," and "play"). Lust, the influence of the basilisk, then, has to be understood as a luxurious play of nature, which allows us to express ourselves and to reflect our souls. On the other hand, it is a form of play which is dangerous and to which we can become addicted. Whether we view it agnostically or religiously, though, the basilisk is always fascinating—just as is the human psyche.

POSTSCRIPT

"So, I am no neatly finished box, I am Man complete with paradox."
Conrad Ferdinand Meyer, 1871

What have we learned from this paradoxical approach to psychology? Have I simply given in to a nihilistic and depressive mind game along the lines of, "there is this and there is that and the end result is nothing?" I hope this is not the case. I hope that I have shown that we psychologists, like all human beings, must have humility. Our knowledge and our awareness of the human soul are terribly limited. The miracle of the soul is far greater than our capacity to grasp it.

Furthermore, the paradoxical approach to psychology illustrates the tragedy of humanity. Rafael Lopez-Pedraza rightly asserts in his paper, "Picasso's Belle Epoque and Blue Period," that our culture has repressed tragic emotions. For this reason, many psychotherapists are incapable of understanding their own conflicts and those of their patients. Tragedy always lies in the paradoxes of the soul, tragedy which no strategy of conflict resolution can eliminate. Tragedy plunges us either into a nihilistic despair or offers us a unique possibility of coming closer to the divine, to the transcendent. I have discussed this aspect in the chapter, *No Answer to Job*.

The paradoxical approach to psychology offers still more. It helps us to play in the most profound sense of the word. Aside from many other things, psychology is also play. This is the case with theology as well. Theology's play varies from the scholastics, with their questions like "How many angels can dance on the head of a pin," to modern feminists who wrestle with problems such as, "Is God male, female, both, or neuter?" Theology's hair-splitting is play for the glory of God; psychology is play for the glory of the soul. We psychologists try to playfully comprehend the soul with images and fables. The paradox of the images reminds us continually that we are playing as if with a kaleidoscope. We shake or turn the images lightly, revealing ever new configurations.

Acknowledging humility, recognizing tragedy, and delighting in play have a healing effect in psychotherapy. Humility helps us to overcome the childish delusions of grandeur which always lead to disappointment. Recognizing the tragic side of our lives does not mean we learn the meaning of life or find the philosopher's stone. That is not possible. Yet, tragedy makes it easier for us to sense the transcendent in life even though, like Job, we understand little of what God says. Recovering our delight in play helps us to rearrange the images and figures of the past, present, and future into new and interesting dramas and novels, tragedies and comedies.

The paradoxical approach to psychology furnishes us with even more. Paradox means something outside of, something contrary to doctrine or general opinion. Paradox does not open, does not quite make sense. These qualities also characterize the soul. Because of its partially acausal autonomy, the soul cannot be forced into any system. For this reason there were understandably calls in the 19th Century for a "psychology without soul," again a paradox. The soul only disturbs. The human soul continually crosses the borders between the rationally and causally ordered world and the other world, the world of the transcendent and the beyond. One of the tasks of the psychotherapist is to help the client to deal with his paradoxes and his madness, even to be glad of them. It is the therapist's task to help the client give up notions of wanting to be a "neatly finished box." The therapist can only do so when he, himself, approaches the paradoxical and contradictory side of his soul.

In the context of the paradox of the soul, I want to refer to something that is perhaps of more interest to the psychologist than to the layman. For about twenty years the diagnosis, "borderline," has played a major role in psychiatry and psychotherapy. "Borderline" refers to a disturbance of psychological development which is characterized by specific symptoms and whose causes are believed to stem from early childhood trauma and wounding. I am interested in the word, "borderline," the line of a border, a limit. Perhaps the popularity of this diagnosis derives from the image suggested by the term. How else could we better characterize the human soul than as "borderline?" As I suggested earlier, we all move between borders. Man with his eternal questions about the meaning of life, with his quixotic striving for consciousness, with his artistic, erotic, and also sexual pretensions and longings places himself continually at the limits, at the borders of earthly existence. The paradoxical side of his being never allows him to rest securely upon the earth. It is not a question of healing the so-called "borderline cases," but of helping those in question to become conscious of their paradoxical, borderline nature.

Is there truly any other approach to psychology other than paradox? In any event, neither the psychotherapist nor the psychologist and in no case the client or the psychological layman should ever demand of themselves that they be a "neatly finished box," but simply— "Man complete with paradox."

A COMMENTARY ON THE WORK AND THOUGHT OF ADOLF GUGGENBÜHL-CRAIG*

SIDNEY HANDEL

"Wherever soul appears, there is secrecy, a secrecy that is expressed through many symbols." ("Money," p. 84)

Prologue

This essay is intended as a review of the writings of Adolf Guggenbühl-Craig. Just as one can hardly describe a corporal life without alluding in some fashion to the psyche that is integral to it, so the study of a corpus of work must refer, finally, to the soul of its author. This necessarily leads of necessity to secrets expressed in 'many symbols.' Some of these are so-called biographical facts—the public record—while others may be inferred from the themes of the works, themselves.

Although familiar with Jung's writings since age sixteen ("Jottings," p. 201), Adolf Guggenbühl-Craig formally entered the Jungian world in 1956. Since that time, he has written a number of articles and books based on Jungian ideas, but meant to appeal to a broader audience. He has presented many more of his innovative ideas as lectures and letters. Most of these ideas have been consolidated into four major works (now five with the present book). These four form the principal subject matter of the present essay with occasional reference to relevant ideas presented only elsewhere. Perhaps, in part, because he wrote these works largely between the ages of forty and sixty, they offer a relatively well-defined set of his issues and concerns. So a review of the "voice" of the writings can be kept within the limits of a few archetypes. If one effect of this approach means a kind of focus through the shadow, then so much the better. As will be seen, much of Guggenbühl-Craig's work has dealt with the shadow and the shadowy aspects of psychological life.

As for the public record, Adolf Guggenbühl-Craig was born on May 25, 1923, in Zürich, Switzerland. Raised in the city where Jung carried on his work, Guggenbühl-Craig became interested in the ideas of Analytical Psychology long before he

*Based on an article originally entitled, "Adolf L. Guggenbühl-Craig e la dimensione dell 'Eros'" in *Psicologia Analitica Contemporanea a cura di Carlo Trombetta* (Milan: Studi Bompiani, pp. 271-310).

finally settled on his profession. From 1942 until 1946, Guggenbühl-Craig attended university where he studied theology, history and philosophy. During these years he also spent time as a social worker. In 1946, he entered medical school to begin his life-long career in psychiatry, psychotherapy and, eventually, Analytical Psychology. These areas of interest, especially theology, social work and healing, continued to be vital concerns in his thinking.

After completing his studies in Zürich and Paris, Guggenbühl-Craig interned in Rhode Island and did his psychiatric residency in Nebraska. Returning to Switzerland, he served as assistant psychiatrist to Manfred Bleuler at Zürich's Burgholzli Clinic (where Jung had done so much of his early work). At the same time, he entered a training analysis with Franz Riklin, the son of Jung's collaborator on the Association Experiment. During the next few years, he completed his analysis, became a Board-certified psychiatrist and opened a private practice in psychiatry, psychotherapy and analysis.

It is one of the ironies (or inner contradictions) of the analytic profession that Freud and Jung, who defined the process, never underwent a personal analysis. In an analogous fashion, Guggenbühl-Craig, who would throughout his Jungian life be so active in the training activity of the C. G. Jung Institute in Zürich, never went through the formal training program. His psychiatric training, his personal studies and his own analysis served to bring him fully into the Jungian world.

During the late 1950's, Guggenbühl-Craig served as advisor to several homes for delinquent boys and girls. At the same time, he frequently acted as expert witness to the court of the Canton of Zürich in criminal cases. These activities expanded his connection to the rank of the helping professions while deepening his knowledge of the darker sides of the psyche.

From the beginning of his formal connection to the Jungian community, he had, in his words, "a great interest in the public life of the Jungians, in the institutional side of the Jungian analysts" (from personal correspondence). He was a member of the Curatorium of the C. G. Jung Institute in Zürich, serving for some years as its president. He then became president of the International Association for Analytical Psychology. After six years in this position, he returned as vice-president to the Curatorium of the Institute.

Marrying in 1950, Guggenbühl-Craig added his wife's name, Craig, to his own following the Swiss custom. He and his wife became the parents of five children and many grandchildren. During the years in which he composed the works under consideration, he maintained an active private practice as well as a vigorous relationship to his several communities of state, church and profession.

One contradiction in Guggenbühl-Craig's life has already been mentioned. Several more should also be touched upon. Chief among them is his abiding interest in group therapy and dynamics, despite the traditional Jungian emphasis on the individual. Indeed the one publication available from his pre-Jungian days, *Gruppenpsychotherapie* (*Group Psychotherapy*), concerns group therapy and it was Guggenbühl-Craig who introduced this approach, against considerable resistance, into the training activities of the Institute in Zürich.

The focus on group activity is important to observe here, because it has implications for the manifestation of *Eros*. An inescapable aspect of group therapy is that so much psyche is carried not only by dream figures, but even more by living human beings. To connect with that psyche involves connecting with the members of the group. This immediately constellates the question of *Eros* — one of the major interests of Guggenbühl-Craig's explorations.

Another contradiction lies in the realm of language. The frequent allusions throughout Guggenbühl-Craig's work to the major nationalistic saga of the Swiss, especially the Swiss-Germans, suggests a passionate patriotism. Every Swiss-German, though, is confronted with a language dilemma. There is a living, dynamic Swiss-German dialect which is a true language of the people. Since it does not exist as a written medium, however, it cannot serve the purpose of formal study. Therefore, Guggenbühl-Craig has to compose in German, which is not his native tongue. Since every translation is also an interpretation, his work is all the more a kind of active imagination — the deepest form of inner contradiction.

As a final word of prologue, it should be said that the real value of Guggenbühl-Craig's works lies in the writings rather than in any commentary on them. Hopefully, any viewpoints expressed here will serve mainly to whet an appetite which only the books and articles could satisfy.

Power Power in the Helping Professions is the study of a major difficulty in those human relations which exist so that one individual may provide assistance to another. Such relationships characterize the disciplines of social work, teaching, medicine and psychotherapy and the ministry. Simply put, the difficulty is that, "The very opposite of what one wants to attain or avoid is repeatedly being constellated" (*Power*, p. 31). Since Jung defined the "shadow" as "the thing a person has no wish to be" (C. G. Jung, *CW* 16, par. 470), it follows that the constellation of the very opposite of what is consciously intended in a helping relationship is a manifestation of the shadow.

One of the many contributions of *Power in the Helping Professions* lies in its differentiation of the general concept of the shadow. Since classical analytical work is with the individual, the shadow has usually been approached from the perspective of the individual ego. Jung generally described shadow as being of the same "stuff" as the ego and Jungians see development of one to follow in tandem with that of the other.

Guggenbühl-Craig begins by broadening the concept of the shadow. He distinguishes a second level that corresponds more to collective than to personal consciousness. This shadow of the "super-ego" corresponds to that which the social setting of a person proscribes as unacceptable. These collective shadow forms develop in the individual as he absorbs the values of his particular social setting that includes family, ethnic group, nation and so forth. This further discrimination of the shadow is particularly useful in understanding relationships between groups. It provides an important background for comprehending the nexus of individual shadow traits and helps to illuminate the source of many unreflected values which are carried individually but are rooted in society. In principle, however, individuals may treat this layer of shadow in the same manner as the personal shadow insofar as its effects on helping relationships are concerned.

There is yet a third distinction of shadow described by Guggenbühl-Craig. This aspect is different not only in degree, but also in kind. Personal and social shadow are clearly relative. What is displeasing or unacceptable to a particular individual or social grouping may not be so to another. Indeed, the evaluation of a shadow phenomenon may be either positive or negative relative to the viewpoint of the observer. This is not so for the third level of shadow, for it is not complementary to ego or social values but to the life principle itself. It corresponds to Freud's notion of *Thanatos* and is characterized by pure destructiveness. The Devil is one personification of this third layer of shadow. From a static perspective, it is really a kind of shadow of the Self, while dynamically it is the negation of the individuation process as understood by Jung.

One could say that every archetype constellates its shadow. As the archetypes form a set of absolutes for the functioning of the psyche, so there is a set of archetypal shadow elements that form an absolute negation of psychological goals and life. As a result of these factors, it must happen that any helping relationship is beset by the difficulties arising from the helper's personal shadow, the shadow of his collective and by an element of pure destructiveness. Complexes, social prejudices and absolute evil are three unavoidable disturbances in the helping professions. Of course, one should expect such disturbances not only in the helping professions, but wherever there is a life of the psyche. Yet, there is a particular way in which they affect the former. To show this, Guggenbühl-Craig develops the concept of the split archetype.

There are, he argues, a number of archetypes that cannot exist without a complementary partner. There is no such thing, in other words, as a Mother Archetype—there is only Mother and Child. There is no such thing as Doctor, Teacher or Minister. There are the sets: Doctor-Patient, Teacher-Student, Minister-Parishioner. These dualities serve as the archetypal underpinnings for the kinds of relationships described in *Power in the Helping Professions*. Ideally, from the perspective of wholeness and consciousness, each individual should realize both poles of these archetypal pairs within himself. More commonly, however, the natural tendency is to split the pair.

The ego remains connected to one of the elements while the other gets projected upon a suitable hook. Indeed, much could be said in favor of this arrangement in terms of natural (i.e., unconscious) development, efficiency and maintenance of the social fabric. At the same time, it is clear that it preserves a large amount of unconscious one-sidedness.

Moreover, the splitting of the archetypal pairs contributes to the destructive possibilities in the helping professions. In analysis, for example, a predominant archetypal configuration is that of the Wounded Healer. This easily leads to a splitting into two parts. There is the fantasy of the conscious, individuating analyst and his unconscious, neurotic patient. The actuality, of course, is that the unconscious, neurotic factors in the analyst get projected onto the analysand while, in symmetrical fashion, the inner healing forces of the analysand are carried by the analyst. For the analyst, this situation is generally far more comfortable than it would be were he to remain in inner contact with his wounds and pains. Thus a powerful, unconscious, incentive to maintain the analysand as the neurotic one becomes constellated.

Guggenbühl-Craig argues that when such a split occurs there is an attempt to close it through power: the one seeking help surrenders power to the Helper. This power, like power in general, is gladly received. At this point it must suffice to note that Guggenbühl-Craig offers no particular justification as to why it should be power and not something else, e.g., *Eros*, that is constellated by the split. He simply asserts it. This issue will be taken up below.

One aspect of Guggenbühl-Craig's creativity lies in the fact that he asks questions about things that one often just takes for granted. One such question has to do with why people enter the helping professions in the first place. The theory of archetypal pairs provides an answer. After all, the choice to spend one's professional life dealing with a particular issue, speaks directly for a fascination with that issue. Naturally, holding only one element of an archetypal pair leaves the other, more difficult one for someone else to carry. The teacher can sustain a fascination with ignorance, while his students carry the ignorance. He can have his cake and eat it, too!

The splitting of the archetypes aggravates these kinds of difficulties by reducing the likelihood of the Helper making them conscious. If he sees all ignorance in the student or all sin in the layman, then the teacher or clergyman can easily remain protected against having to take responsibility for his share. The maintenance of defenses prevents the only antidote, namely consciousness, from serving its function. Awareness of a shared problem, for example, can effect a positive movement in the analytical situation. The projection of the analyst's neurosis onto his patient, on the other hand, diminishes the chances of such an awareness.

As an alternative, Guggenbühl-Craig proposes that the best means to avoid the problem of becoming ensnared in shadow projections is to have the helper be deeply touched by forces against which he cannot easily defend himself. This happens best in the meaningful *Eros* connections one develops in the real, non-professional world — the world of friends, lovers, mates and children. Guggenbühl-Craig makes an essential connection here among the factors of shadow, power, *Eros* and individuation.

According to Guggenbühl-Craig, one should not see all ideas about another person, even in the analytical situation, as projection. There are also real visions of the other. These are the fantasies whose origin derives from the essential reality of the person. They include not only glimpses of the individual as he is, but also intimations of possibilities for the future. Thus they may be creative or destructive. Most important, however, is that projections originate from the observer's psyche while visions stem from the reality of the one observed. This perception serves as a corrective to the temptation to make Jung's theory a sophisticated solipsism. For, if one can grasp the other through those visions that are truly a part of him and not just projected, then real, non-transferential relationship becomes both possible and, for psychic health, necessary.

This perspective also underlines Guggenbühl-Craig's belief that ultimately psychotherapy is an "erotic activity" (*Power*, p. 71): it is based upon the possibility of connecting to the patient as he truly is. Together with the importance he attributes to *Thanatos*, this reintroduction of *Eros* into the analytic process speaks to a special kind of connection to Freud's ideas that will be pursued below. Here it is sufficient to observe that, in his discussion of the topic, Guggenbühl-Craig takes sexuality out of its narrow Freudian constrictions, for he characterizes it as primarily relational rather than pleasure-oriented or reproductive.

Finally, one might note that Jungian writers have not generally accepted the theory of split archetypes to the same degree as they have many of Guggenbühl-Craig's other ideas. This is because much of the thinking that has developed from this conceptual approach can be derived directly from traditional shadow theory. It is, however, crucial for understanding Guggenbühl-Craig's work since it focuses attention on personifications rather than reifications. Relationship with another human being, not only unconscious imagery, takes the place of the other pole of an archetypal split. In conjunction with the emphasis on the erotic nature of the helping relationship, the importance of personification highlights the pre-eminence of *Eros* in Guggenbühl-Craig's work.

Connection

Power in The Helping Professions is an exploration of the limits faced in the attempt to do social good. Guggenbühl-Craig sees power as a destructive symptom of a common problem in the work. He suggests an "erotic" confrontation (i.e., involving *Eros*) outside the professional work as a way to avoid or, at least, minimize the difficulty. Guggenbühl-Craig's second major work, *Marriage — Dead or Alive*, explores the institution of matrimony, probably the most common arena of the *Eros* confrontation.

Looking at this work as it stands for the moment, the problem it addresses may be simply stated. The fantasy of the happy marriage is apparently quite dead. The disastrous state of the institution as measured by divorce rates as well as the negative, collective image it enjoys, gives weight to the idea that it is a tottering edifice awaiting only a better system of child care before it ultimately collapses. Guggenbühl-Craig confronts this dark reality and demonstrates that it holds an enormous reservoir of psychological energy.

He begins with a discussion of the differences between

the archetype of marriage and the many, complex forms in which that archetype manifests. These forms are, so to speak, the "images" of marriage. Guggenbühl-Craig shows how these are so often "unnatural." He comes to the general conclusion that marriage is, in fact, an *opus contra naturam*. His choice of phrase is not accidental. It is the same term used by Jung to describe the individuation process, because the thesis of *Marriage – Dead or Alive* is that marriage is, or can be, an individuation process.

Guggenbühl-Craig makes a distinction between the marriage of "well-being" and the marriage of "salvation." By well-being he means a relative absence of unpleasant tensions, the satisfaction of instinctual needs and material desires and the fulfillment of social needs such as companionship and a sense of community. The happy marriage is a marriage of well-being. While it may be that such a marriage was always more likely to exist in fantasy than in reality, the western world has believed the fantasy as a true possibility until modern times. Compensatory negative elements found their main expression in jokes, gossip and fiction. At the present time, however, one can hardly entertain even the fantasy. As Guggenbühl-Craig observes, the marital context seems better designed to be a torture chamber than a pleasure palace. The marriage of well-being is "dead."

By "salvation" Guggenbühl-Craig refers to the general notion of seeking and finding God. This would correspond, in psychological terms, to the ego's seeking and finding connection to the Self. Yet, Guggenbühl-Craig has already defined the relationship of ego and Self in idiosyncratic manner as individuation (*Power*, p. 139). If marriage is a context which makes the ego-Self connection possible, the marriage of salvation is very much alive, in sharp distinction to the marriage of well-being. Marriage, then, is as alive as the general possibility of individuation.

Already in *Power in the Helping Professions*, Guggenbühl-Craig had presented some characteristics of individuation such as its definition and its non-elitist character. One should consider several additional points here. First, for Guggenbühl-Craig, individuation is not a time-bound process. It is an experience that can be happening at any stage of a person's life and it is episodic rather than progressive. Second, it is not equivalent to "mental health." It may not involve either the relief of symptoms or the end of unhappiness. This understanding of individuation, of course, makes it all the more possible to find it in marriage, an experience of youth as well as old age, of misery as well as joy.

One might misunderstand this characterization of individuation (as contact between ego and Self) just as the parallel religious image of a connection between man and God so often is—as an angelic, spiritually shadowless experience. Guggenbühl-Craig sees the process in terms which are not only radically different but which also serve as a link between his first two books. For what he means by the individuation process is the constellation of "courage, cowardice, active fighting, filth and the gruesome" (*Marriage*, p. 29) rather than a spiritually elegant journey.

The joining of opposites, so well symbolized by man and woman, involves "coming to terms with suffering and death, with the dark side of God and his creation, with what makes us suffer, with what we use to torment ourselves and others . . . There can be no individuation without confrontation with the destructiveness of God, of the world and of our own soul." (*Marriage*, p. 31). Guggenbühl-Craig supports this position by his agreement with Jung that individuation is not individualism and always involves the need to struggle with or relate to others. Marriage makes an excellent, if not always pleasant, container for this need.

This "salvational" aspect of marriage has led to its celebration as a universally enacted religious sacrament, absent only in cultures which politically ban such sacraments. This is because religious ritual always marks the archetypal events— the "stations" on the path of natural life and the "stations" on the path of individuation. Only two other areas match the social energy given to marriage celebration rituals, namely, birth and death (the two points of inevitable connection between natural existence and an *opus contra naturam*).

Lest one mistake what may be a possibility for a necessity, Guggenbühl-Craig makes it clear that, for many individuals, marriage is inappropriate. Their way lies elsewhere. Equally important is the fact that any particular marriage may fail to carry the process. From a long-range psychological perspective, such a marriage may end without great loss.

Of course, many marriages *do* end even though they could serve the goal of individuation. One apparent reason is that traditional marriage has, in the Western world, been associated with the suppression of much of the feminine. In actuality, a number of the archetypal possibilities for women have little to do with relating to men. These include the amazon, the priestess and many others. Other archetypal aspects of the feminine such as lover, companion, or mother, have dominated marriage. As the realization has finally dawned that all of these, the former as well as the latter, are potentials for all women, Western society has come to experience marriage ever more sharply as an institution in which the sacrifice of so much of the feminine is too great. The culture has come to perceive the death of marriage as one of the requirements for the liberation of women. The marriage of individuation is clearly no longer compatible with such a wholesale restriction of feminine development. Guggenbühl-Craig argues that the living marriage must encompass many archetypal models of partnership, including those that promise either no connection between man and woman or only a hostile one. Guggenbühl-Craig generalizes this idea to the conclusion that the marriage of individuation must allow room for the energies that flow from archetypal conflicts within each individual as well as from those between the partners. These inner, archetypal conflicts, however, are also what generate the neuroses. This is another way of saying that a marriage, to be alive, must contain and struggle with its neurotic components. Put even more strongly, Guggenbühl-Craig argues that a neurotic marriage may very well be an individuating, living relationship.

Here, again, he stands the inescapable upon its head. He recognizes that marriages are inherently neurotic — a recognition that, when made by others, has usually led to condemnation of the institution. Guggenbühl-Craig reaches the opposite conclusion. For the individual, the struggle to deal with irreconcilable opposites generates the development of psyche. Individuation, in other words, is made possible through the tensions caused by the neurotic aspects of the personality. This is also true in marriage when the inclusion of neurotic factors results in confrontations with the other (and with the unconscious) that can lead to contact between ego and Self. This remarkable idea, both simple and profound, connects immediately with another area of tremendous import.

The vision of marriage as container of the neurotic opens up the general question of sexuality, disturbances of which the Freudian perspective holds to be both cause and result of neurosis. Guggenbühl-Craig offers a number of innovative insights into the nature of human sexuality. Primary is his observation that the overwhelming majority of sexual activity takes place in the psyche, in fantasy, with relatively little ever manifested in overt sexuality. Moreover, the forms that sexual imagination takes are often of the sort that one might consider perverse. Much, even most, of the sexuality that is lived out does not meet the criterion of "normality" as understood by the traditional prejudices of psychology or religion. Most sexuality, in other words, has little or no connection with reproduction and much is not even genitally organized. At the extreme, a great deal of human sexual energy has little to do in any direct sense with either union or pleasure: "Neither procreation, nor pleasure, nor interpersonal relation ship explains the enormous variety of sexual life and sexual fantasy." (*Marriage*, p. 80)

When one takes the ritualization of sexuality into account, along with the numinosity that accompanies it, the conclusion seems to be both inescapable and startling. "Sexuality, with all its variations, can be understood as an individuation fantasy. . . " (*Marriage*, p. 82). All the factors which seem to so complicate sexual reality join to form a meaningful whole when regarded as indications of an individuation drama.

Clearly, the idea of "normal sexuality" becomes as meaningless as would be a concept of "normal" individuation — a contradiction in terms. In a sense, human sexuality is fundamentally neurotic, being so separated from its reproductive origins. Rather than being only a problem, as Freud imagined, one may see this as an opportunity for the full realization of what is especially human. Marriage, as the focus of so much sexual activity (and frustration) is one important place where this may happen.

Naturally, the more that each partner's sexuality can be allowed in the marriage, the more likely is psychological movement. One should not understand this naively. First, many people may simply not have much sexual interest. Also, how any particular sexual energy manifests itself must be determined within the particular context: "(o)ne would . . . try not to evade the other sexually just as one would not evade the other psychologically. . . Just how this is lived out is the business of each individual married couple and of each partner" (*Marriage*, p. 101). Most important, however, is the idea that the confrontation with sexuality does not necessarily mean its concretization. "The sacrifice of sexuality is just as meaningful as its enactment" (*Marriage*, p. 113). With this observation, Guggenbühl-Craig returns to the general issue of marriage.

Sacrifice is a question one cannot avoid in considering any marriage. Fear that the necessary sacrifices of marriage may be more than the Self can bear, has led to the sometimes expressed, sometimes implicit, analytic view that married people cannot individuate. On the contrary, argues Guggenbühl-Craig, sacrifice in and for marriage can be, as is sacrifice for the individual, a necessary aspect of growth. So while there are some whose development must lie outside of marriage, there are others for whom marriage, even unhappy marriage, is a pathway to individuation.

Limitation

In *Power in the Helping Professions*, Guggenbühl-Craig proposed that a strong *Eros* relationship, experienced apart from the work, is crucial for the therapist. *Marriage – Dead or Alive* explores what is probably the most common and important example of such a relationship. Continuing a preoccupation with the dark side of the Self, Guggenbühl-Craig's third major work, *Eros on Crutches*, focuses on the problems constellated when *Eros* is crippled.

He introduces the subject with a description of a problem encountered in medicine. Modern times have witnessed a nearly complete victory over bacterial infections, significant strides toward the prevention of (many) viral diseases and enormous advances in technology with concomitant surgical benefits. Nevertheless, to practice medicine is to confront what appears to be a core of the incurable, a fundamental inability to heal. True, much of what medicine cannot heal turns out to be psychological in nature, but this only takes the problem one level deeper. For psychology, too, despite the introduction of psychopharmaceuticals, has met very real and constraining limits on its ability to heal. Lack of wholeness, the inability to be healed, appears to be a chronic problem.

Here, again, Guggenbühl-Craig sees through the manifest difficulty to the underlying mysteries of the Self. Rather than continuing to focus on the failure of healing — a focus which implies the hero archetype — he looks instead for the spirit which informs the psyche's attachment to the chronically problematic. It is, he claims, archetypal! Just as there is a drive towards restoration, cure and health — a homeostasis of body and soul — so there is a corresponding *daimon* (i.e., archetype) of invalidism. Since this *daimon* opposes the drive towards wholeness, one might expect it to always "act" against the individuation process in order to maintain a chronic state of deficiency. Being archetypal, invalidism is autonomous! By this, Guggenbühl-Craig means that it is free from necessary ties to outer, concrete reality. So no matter how healthy the body nor how vigorous the life of the imagination, every individual may be in touch with the experience of being crippled.

Guggenbühl-Craig is deliberate in his choice of the words, "invalid," "cripple" and "chronic." For he does not mean to speak here of illness and disease: they may be cured or they may kill. They have a goal. "Invalidism, however, leads nowhere, neither to death nor to health. It is a lasting deficiency" (*Eros*, p. 17). One might argue that chronicity is simply the shadow of growth. Yet, Guggenbühl-Craig deliberately seeks to have it stand on what he might have called its "one good leg." He presents it as one part of an archetypal pair that cultural, personal and, possibly, evolutionary biases have separated from its companion. This formulation follows the model of the split archetype established in *Power in the Helping Professions*.

He goes on to express the thought that the fantasy in medicine and psychology in favor of health and wholeness leads to an attitude of moral superiority in therapists towards those who suffer from psychosomatic disorders or neuroses in general. From this notion, one may derive an answer to the question posed above as to why a split archetype should constellate power rather than, say, *Eros*. For the assumption of moral superiority would discourage the flow of true *Eros* which always requires, more or less, the acceptance of the other as he is! The void thus created could well be filled by power which operates only when the possibilities of "superior" and "inferior" are active. Returning to Guggenbühl-Craig's exposition, one might see that elevating the phenomenon of invalidism to a relatively independent status allows, even demands, that it be examined on its terms. This, in turn, permits that continued confrontation with darkness that is so integral to Guggenbühl-Craig's understanding of individuation. This has several implications. For one thing, although the word "invalid" derives from the Latin word meaning "weak," the invalid, himself, is not necessarily so. This is only logical since, by definition, the archetype is the repository or source of psychic energy. Weakness may be archetypal, but an archetype, itself, cannot be without energy.

Of course, the tyranny of the invalid is a well-known motif. This notion refers to a form of passive-aggressiveness. Also well known, is the capacity of an invalid to constellate the need to help in another. This is another form of the power of weakness. Guggenbühl-Craig, however, refers to a third, more independent kind of strength of the invalid. He shows that the invalid may, despite the invalidism, demonstrate a life strength and general competence. This could be the result of an Adlerian compensation. It may, instead, be the reflection of one way in which the ego comes to terms with chronicity, just as it must do with the other archetypes.

Two other conclusions flow from accepting the Invalid as a "valid" archetype. First, being archetypal, it is part of wholeness. Therefore, completeness must contain the incomplete, since individuation must include the consciousness and integration of the crippled aspects of the psyche. Second and closely related, the acceptance of invalidism as archetypal removes the absolute demand for cure. Therapy or analysis need not attempt to overcome all deficiencies. Efforts to assist the sufferer may also consist of finding ways for him to grant legitimacy to his disabilities.

This, of course, is an idea similar to that of accepting a problem on its terms, the *sine qua non* of differentiation, which along with individuation, is the hallmark of psychological development. For example, Jungians generally agree that an archetype, in and of itself, is neither good nor bad, neither pleasant nor unpleasant. Its value as a subjective entity depends on several other factors such as its relationship to the ego.

But Guggenbühl-Craig focuses on another area concerning the valence of an archetype. Not surprisingly, given what has already been said, he asserts that it ". . . is *Eros* who makes the archetypes loving, creative and involved" (*Eros*, p. 27). The invalid can be tyrannical, egotistical and life-denying in the absence of *Eros*. He can evoke warmth in others and exude it himself if *Eros* is present. On the inner level, invalidism can stir philosophical or moral speculation, leading to wisdom, or it can result in a stultifying bitterness. All depends upon the presence or absence of *Eros*! Guggenbühl-Craig goes even further when he claims that the ". . . presence or absence of relationship among archetypes in an individual is the determining factor for his character and his fate. This relationship depends on *Eros*. . . " (*Eros*, p. 28).

Making an implicit question overt, Guggenbühl-Craig asks what happens when the archetypes of *Eros* and the Invalid become intertwined rather than simply related. What is the situation, that is, when an individual's capacity to experience *Eros* becomes crippled? Then, he argues, there is psychopathy! As has already been observed, Guggenbühl-Craig's conception of individuation is such that it requires confrontation with the dark, destructive forces of life and psyche. The figure of the psychopath is the ideal personification of these negative energies. It is for this reason that the psychopath figures so prominently in Guggenbühl-Craig's interests, despite the fact that, as he acknowledges, the classical concept of psychopathy is now rather outdated in medicine and psychology.

Indeed, much of *Eros on Crutches* is devoted to a masterful depiction of the image of the psychopath. For even if psychopathy has diminished in importance as a diagnostic category, the image of the psychopath continues to exert a fascination for both the individual and collective psyche. This, in turn, can only be true if the image continues to serve as the personification of an experiential reality: ". . . it seems that the psychological importance of psychopathy is the extent to which it stimulates the fantasy and imagination . . . " (*Eros*, p. 67). It is the image of the psychopath that stimulates *Eros on Crutches*.

Guggenbühl-Craig explores in detail the history and usage of the term psychopathy in psychiatry and psychology. In the process, he raises the question of etiology. The issue is whether psychopaths are born as such or are "created" by their social nexus. Put intra-psychically, are the empty, amoral places in each psyche part of its inheritance or the result of the individual's life history? This question seems almost archaic to many modern readers (especially, according to Guggenbühl-Craig, those of the political left) since they cherish the fantasy of the psyche as a tabula rasa. The issue of nature versus nurture remains an area of general uncertainty where proof is difficult to come by. Naturally, one can give no definitive answer. Yet, posing the question, itself, is of value. For one thing, it challenges the widespread modern mythologem that all individuals are born equal, especially morally. (The discussion of the next work will address this mythologem more fully.)

Given the image of psychopathy, Guggenbühl-Craig proceeds to differentiate it. He first describes what he calls the five primary symptoms that are found in all cases of psychopathy. They are the inability to love, a missing or deficient sense of morality, the absence of psychological development, background depression and chronic, low-level fear. He describes each of these symptoms in depth and shows how each results from a basic lack of *Eros*. Consider the deficient sense of morality as one example.

Guggenbühl-Craig argues that what one terms morality is, in the end, a kind of substitute for the inner constellation of *Eros*. When *Eros* is present, so to speak, there is no need for morality. *Eros*, itself, works for the greatest degree of relationship in the situation. Even when no basic problem exists, there are moments or contexts when *Eros* is missing. It is in those moments that the individual motivated by a sense of *Eros* will substitute a moral code. Morality is a way of institutionalizing the positive results of *Eros* whose evocation, like that of any archetype, is essentially beyond the full control of the ego. The psychopath does not know *Eros* and, therefore, cannot and need not know morality. Guggenbühl-Craig discusses all of the five primary symptoms with similar conclusions. He shows each to be the expression of a missing or inadequate connection to *Eros*.

Tangential to the question of an *Eros* deficiency, Guggenbühl-Craig raises two points. First, he asks, can the psychopath have a truly religious experience? Without being able to explain it, Guggenbühl-Craig claims that, based on his empirical observation, the answer is a clear, "yes." This is another way of saying that the Self is recognizable also in the psychopath. This assertion implies the paradoxical conclusion that, although he has little or no psychological development, the psychopath can still experience individuation, the contact between ego and Self. This highlights the idiosyncratic nature of Guggenbühl-Craig's view of individuation which, in some respects, varies greatly from Jung's.

Second, there is the question of the psychopath's relationship to sexuality. Of course, lacking *Eros*, the psychopath is unable to experience sexuality as the deepest connection between human beings. Nevertheless, Guggenbühl-Craig observes, the sexual life of the psychopath is ". . . not subject to neurotic complications which, in the final analysis, result from erotic difficulties" (*Eros*, p. 95). This is a remarkable statement for a Jungian and its implications will be discussed in some detail later.

Along with the primary symptoms that characterize all psychopathy, there are a number of secondary symptoms which serve to distinguish its various specific forms. These include, among others, such things as an absence of guilt, lack of insight, a certain type of charm and, occasionally, asocial or criminal behavior. For these, too, Guggenbühl-Craig identifies an absence or deficiency of *Eros* as causal. Problematically, one encounters many of these symptoms in situations where the underlying cause is not a crippled *Eros*. Guggenbühl-Craig illustrates this by presenting four cases with a diagnosis of psychopathy. In only two of them is it an appropriate designation. In the other two, the individuals are either operating out of a different social nexus than their observers or are being consistent with a variant, but realistic, internal set of values. One must, it seems, apply the term, "psychopathy," with care.

The psychopath's ability to compensate for his *Eros* deficiency presents another problem. By compensation, Guggenbühl-Craig means, " . . . balancing a psychic defect through special effort" (*Eros*, p.106). This effort may be conscious or unconscious. A common form of compensation for amorality is the adoption of an excessively rigid moral code. One such compensation is the choice of a career persona where morality, the substitute for *Eros*, is a structural part of the work. Therefore, "(w)e should not . . . be surprised to find large numbers of compensated psychopaths in the so-called 'helping professions': teaching, psychiatry, the ministry, social work and the like" (*Eros*, p. 107). It is self-evident, of course, that psychopathy can only be a further factor contributing to the difficulties, already discussed, of power abuse in those professions.

Another form of compensation is available through negative social reinforcement. So, for example, all the Nazi concentration camp functionaries, all of Stalin's subordinates who cooperated in the various Soviet purges, all of those who assisted in the destruction of large portions of Chinese society during Mao's regime, "certainly all of these people were compensated psychopaths" (*Eros*, p. 108).

At this point, it begins to become clear that. in talking about the compensated psychopath, Guggenbühl-Craig seems to be referring to everyone except the Saint. He makes explicit that there is no "us" or "them" with psychopathy. There is only the question of how each individual compensates for his areas of *Eros* deficiency.

If, however, nearly every personality has psychopathic elements, why is there not even more destructiveness in the world than is already experienced, individually and collectively? To answer this, Guggenbühl-Craig returns to the theme of the shadow as developed in *Power in the Helping Professions*. He argues that the tension between a destructive core of shadow, or *Thanatos* and an equally matched *Eros*, is the source of creativity. A deficiency of *Eros* ensures the relative dominance of *Thanatos*, but the latter's absolute strength is another matter. The psychopath, that is, need not have an especially strong shadow and, therefore, need not be particularly destructive — although the relatively rare individual who is receives much fascinated attention. Again, viewed intra-psychically, the psychopathic elements in the individual psyche may, but generally need not, lead to destructive behavior by that individual.

At the collective level, things are more difficult. Since the psychopath enjoys freedom from the constraints imposed by *Eros*, he is in a relatively advantageous position to achieve power in society. Indeed, Guggenbühl-Craig ascribes psychopathy to many of history's most influential figures. He points to an almost absolute necessity for each society to cast a cold eye upon its heroes. Since such vigilance is so difficult and unusual, one must conclude that psychopathy may be the dominant feature in the dark political landscape depicted by Guggenbühl-Craig. Yet, as he asserts, "We are all, as I will repeatedly insist, partially psychopaths" (*Eros*, p.105).

What is to be done with this subjective, partial psychopathy? The Saint, according to Guggenbühl-Craig, has no need of morality since he is always in full touch with *Eros*. The pure psychopath also has no need for morality, since, not knowing *Eros*, he cannot know its substitute. Between the poles of Saint and psychopath, however, lies the space where *Eros* and morality are interchangeable substitutes for each other. While, the *Eros* connection is certainly preferable, it is never fully accessible for most individuals. The treatment of partial psychopathy, subjective or objective, lies in filling the gap left by an absence of *Eros* with morality — personal or social codes of prescribed correct behavior and attitude. With a measure of psychological humility, Guggenbühl-Craig ends his monograph with the suggestion that there is nothing wrong with providing morality's crutch for the one-legged man in each of us.

Debilitation In his discussion of invalidism, Guggenbühl-Craig remarks that if individuals were born with various psychic lacunae already present, it would threaten the cherished notion that "all men are created equal." *The Old Fool and the Corruption of Myth* begins with a detailed discussion of this notion of equality.

Marshaling sociological, psychological and historical data, Guggenbühl-Craig makes a devastating critique of the idea of innate equality. Much of the evidence for his position is immediately available to any observer. Much also seems intuitively clear. Yet, the belief not only persists, it dominates the current perception of society so fully that to hold an opposite view is to invite contempt. In practical terms, the belief in equality is a determining standard both for revolutionary movements and the measure in world opinion for all societies.

His discussion of the tenacity of this belief provides the context for the themes of *The Old Fool and the Corruption of Myth*. For, behind this idea whose effect is to break down barriers and categories, he glimpses the figure of Dionysos. Whether it be Dionysian energy exactly, he observes, is less important than the overall notion that something archetypal informs the belief in equality and that it is, therefore, a modern mythologem! This one, of course, has many positive aspects.

Guggenbühl-Craig goes on to discuss how specific mythologems drive or lead nations, families and individuals. In many instances, these also affect the group or individual in a positive way, serving both physical and psychological life. Some, however, are pernicious and destructive. Such, for example, was the case for the mythological frenzy of the German nation in the recent past. This radical example may be matched on a more mundane level by instances in which individuals or families display patterns of thought or behavior that are mythogically driven. When viewed from outside, though, they resemble neurotic, self-limiting or even self-destructive syndromes. Because of this destructive aspect and in keeping with the collective mythologem of "rationalism" (predominant since the Age of Enlightenment), the last several centuries have been, until very recent times, an age of demythologizing.

It is one of Jung's great contributions that he restored the mythological dimension to the study of the psyche. Indeed, Analytical Psychology accepts the process of mythologizing as the fundamental basis of soul work. Through myths individual and collective psyches express and reveal themselves. One example is the tale of William Tell, which best expresses a fundamental, yet mythological, reality of the Swiss nation. Yet, the national reality of Switzerland is only partial just as other modern mythologems such as "economic man" or "the narcissistic culture" express a reality, albeit not the reality. Since mythologems are only partial and sometimes destructive as well, psychology's need for them creates a great danger. There is a need, therefore, to understand what it is that does make some mythologems destructive.

Guggenbühl-Craig offers two primary explanations. First, there is one-sidedness. A mythologem whose complement is not carried in a competing but legitimate fashion, is apt to be dangerous. A constellation of opposites within the psyche holding the myth is necessary to curb the excesses of one-sidedness. A clear example of this is, again, National Socialism where no inner sense of inferiority existed to compensate the ideology of racial superiority. Instead, Nazism projected the inferiority fully outward with catastrophic results. The one-sided mythologem, by virtue of its incompleteness, is potentially negative. Examples abound and Guggenbühl-Craig presents a number of them.

The second source of destructiveness results from a failure to draw a sharp enough distinction between what is appropriate for the gods and what is appropriate for humans. The two are often very different, but may be confused because of the basic nature of myths. They are, so to speak, a bridge between men and gods or, in psychological terms, an avenue of communication between ego and archetype. On the immortal side of the bridge, the terms of understanding and behavior are necessarily different from those on the mortal side. It is the confusion between the rules of each realm which lies at the root of the evil of antinomianism.

A simple illustration of the point is the mythologem of the brother-sister marriage. Jung has shown this not uncommon heavenly motif to be symbolic of basic dynamisms in the individuation process. Its concretization, however, is generally disastrous. Even the ancient Egyptians permitted the ritual of brother-sister marriage only when they considered the celebrants to be true incarnations of the gods.

To set the stage for the second part of his discussion,

Guggenbühl-Craig turns to a particular example of a one-sided, dangerous mythologem, namely the fantasy of continual progress. It is of special relevance for him because it plays such a large role even in Jung's psychology. Jung's image of the individuation process is as a kind of spiral which, despite its circling, maintains a forward motion. The ego's encounter with the forces in the unconscious psyche follows a definite progression. It begins as a struggle with the shadow and moves, finally, to a meeting with the wise, old man/woman as a representative of the (mature) Self. One element that makes this mythologem pernicious is the one-sided implication that old age is the repository of wisdom.

Before proceeding to explore the particular mythologem of old age and wisdom, Guggenbühl-Craig pauses to make a point characteristic of his perception of psyche. He observes that the antidote to a dangerous one-sidedness is a continual connection to the inner contradictions of the psyche. This is striking because, again, it reverses the obvious. Remaining in touch with his inner contradictions is extremely difficult for the individual, especially if he would not be neurotic. Neurosis is the compromise achieved from the collision of two nearly equal but conflicting psychological attitudes. To praise the inner contradiction is very close to paying homage to neurosis. As this discussion will show, it is instead homage to individuation.

Guggenbühl-Craig turns to the theme that gives this monograph is title. Old age, he argues, has historically attracted two contradictory sets of images. We see it on the one hand as a blessing and on the other as a curse. The fantasy of the senior citizen surrounded by a loving family represents the blessed side. The youngest members come for the undemanding love they know they will receive, while their older relatives stand ready to profit from the sage advice of the experienced and trusted elder. The lonely, sick, mentally enfeebled and bitter individual whose continued care is a source of resentment for all concerned, personifies the curse.

There are, of course, certain inescapable and unpleasant aspects of aging. They are unavoidable. Despite this, the image of the positive and blessed side persists. The fantasy defies rational analysis and neither appeals to the value of experience nor the imagined progressive nature of individuation seem to affect it. Nor can it be fully explained as compensation. It is an ideal example of a modern mythologem. As a one-sided mythologem, however and one where what goes well for the gods does not for humans, it is destructive. It negates what might, instead, be a good way to enter and experience old age. Also, it makes demands, objective and subjective, which are cruel by virtue of the impossibility of their being satisfied.

In counterpoint to this mythologem, Guggenbühl-Craig offers another that he claims to be far healthier. This is the notion of the old fool! The old fool is one who accepts and even embraces the diminution of mental, physical and social capacities. The image of the old fool has a traditional basis and its value lies in the freedom attained by the letting go of the demands of wisdom, power and importance. Its benefit is that of withdrawal. Since the old fool is where the core of the Self arrives in old age, individuation lies in connecting with the condition of being without energy for the world. This attitude leaves the old fool free to be a fool, to speak, act and dress as he will without fear of offending or appearing badly in the eyes of others.

PERSPECTIVES

Adolf Guggenbühl-Craig's first publication, a study of group therapy, appeared as part of a series devoted to the study of child development. His last, prior to this publication, is principally a study of old age. The continuity of the path between childhood and old age, the poles of earthly existence, seems very clear. Along that path, one typically encounters the questions of earning a living, establishing a family and coming to terms with limitations. These are the implicit themes of the works just discussed. The sequence of power, connection, limitation and debilitation could also describe the life cycle of an individual.

Power in the Helping Professions was published in 1971, when its author was forty-eight years old. It incorporates the ideas of several of his earlier articles: "The Psychotherapist's Shadow," "Medicine and Power," "Analytical Rigidity" and "Must Analysis Fail." The author developed those ideas during the last years of the 1960's when he was in his forties. He wrote it from the perspective of an individual who has had to deal with the effects of his considerable power on his environment and on himself. Many of those effects, of course, are shadowy. For this reason, the Shadow is, in some sense, the main topic of the book. As explained in *Eros on Crutches,* whether the shadow's destructive capacities become manifest depends upon the absence or presence of *Eros.* To a direct extent, then, whether the helping professions create harm while consciously seeking its opposite depends on their finding a way to maintain a good connection to *Eros.*

Even more important, though, is the indirect influence of *Eros.* Because of the inherent strength of the defenses of his position, the one in the helping role is liable to have too effective a shield for his complexes. This maintains a kind of unconsciousness, which not only harms his clients, but also inhibits his own psychological life. Guggenbühl-Craig contends that *Eros,* found in relationships outside the work area, is the best agent for breaking through this defense and letting in new light. Increased consciousness can then mitigate the negative possibilities through a greater awareness of shadow. In an effort to protect against the excesses of inner and outer power, Guggenbühl-Craig appeals to *Eros.* For the culture in which these works were written and are read, the main carrier of *Eros* for most people is marriage.

For some reason, Analytical Psychology has often incorporated *Eros* as something nice, even sweet. As a result, any alternative view requires a more elaborate argument than it otherwise would. In his pursuit of marital *Eros,* Guggenbühl-Craig must first deal with the unpleasant reality that so much of the marriage experience is negative or, at least, subjectively felt to be so. An understanding of the subtleties of the shadow is crucial in comprehending how the results of the helping professions may go awry. The necessities of the individuation process are key to grasping the real possibilities of marriage.

In his description of individuation, Guggenbühl-Craig makes it quite clear that one does not experience the break up of defenses alluded to in *Power in the Helping Professions* as a pleasure. Moreover, his vision of individuation focuses on a need for there to be a real connection to the dark and destructive sides of life and Self. In other words, the marriage with individuation potential may also be one in which the partners are very far away indeed from "living happily ever after." If discomfort, suffering and sacrifice need not be inimical to *Eros* or to individuation, though, there are other factors that might be.

Marriage – Dead or Alive was composed and published during the first few years of the fifth decade of the author's life. Involved with the questions of love, marriage and family, it deals with issues that belong, together with those presented in *Power in the Helping Professions*, to what Jung described as the first stage of life. He wrote it from the perspective of a man who has turned his attention away from the profession to an area where neurosis and love complicate the question of what is true power. It is optimistic in the sense that, despite its visions of difficulties, it stands for a belief in the movement of psyche and of an obtainable individuation.

Eros on Crutches marks the author's transition into the second half of his fifties and, probably, into the second half of life as well. Written with a darker tone than was sounded in *Marriage – Dead or Alive*, it begins with the proposition that everything in the reality of life, including the human psyche, is deficient in some regard. Granted that *Eros* is necessary to guard against the abuse of power, to keep psychic life astir and to defend against the excesses of shadow elements, what if the human deficiency lies in the quarter of *Eros*? Worse, what if *Eros* is crippled, to some extent at least? Then marriage, of course, meets some real limitations. More significantly, psyche encounters the psychopath.

Just as struggling with the shadow is so necessary for individuation, so wrestling with psychopathy is an inescapable facet of dealing with the vicissitudes of *Eros*. The conclusion of *Eros on Crutches* is clear: Every psyche, save that of the Saint, contains its *Eros* inadequacies and, therefore, must deal with its own psychopathy. Because *Eros* must occasionally fail, the human being must rely repeatedly on the rules of morality to bridge the resulting emptiness. Doing this is a difficult and burdensome task, but a lack of success is even worse, especially if the failure belongs to powerful neighbors. *Eros on Crutches* reflects the situation of a man who recognizes a problem and visualizes a solution to it. In the end, however, Guggenbühl-Craig sees the problem to be chronic and the solution to exist only in theory. This, in turn, implies that the tension between *Thanatos* and *Eros* is bound to overflow its container with destructive results. It is the case that ". . . out of the admixture of the two, destruction and renewal, comes something creative, comes THE Creative" (*Eros*, p. 113). In the progress of life, however, there must also come, again and again, something that negates that creativity. The ego remains suspended in the tension of these opposites.

Guggenbühl-Craig wrote *The Old Fool and the Corruption of Myth* soon after he entered his sixties, an event of considerable moment in European culture. It supposedly signifies the crossing of the threshold into the youth of old age. Properly, then, it takes the issue of power and *Eros* to its conclusion. What *The Old Fool* presents is not the image of the wise old man steering the ego, the family, or the nation down the path of individuation and development, sagely avoiding the obstacles of power and shadow. On the contrary, the privilege of old age is the withdrawal of concern! *Power* is surrendered just in equal measure to the removal of libido from the world. To put it another way, *Eros* and power surrender their sovereignty together. This frees the old fool to play his role—a King Lear content with his discontent. The perspective is of giving up, of pulling back and of loss.

So Guggenbühl-Craig has moved from having too much power, through the struggle to moderate its effects, up to the point where that power comes to a natural end. This depiction of the struggle with power, the turn towards *Eros*, the recognition of inherent limitations and inadequacies and the final retreat to involution, would seem to lend itself to a dark, gloomy and defeatist mood. Oddly, however, the experience of following this process through Guggenbühl-Craig's writings is anything but negative. Psyche is shocked and surprised, but also stimulated and relieved somehow of the heavy burden of its wounds, failures and discontents. This is surely another example of inner contradiction. Yet, how is it so?

The answer lies in Guggenbühl-Craig's unique conception of the individuation process. Ironically, the progression of the narrator/ego through the four monographs, represents the classical Jungian journey. There is the confrontation with the shadow, the union with the anima/animus, the dark night of the soul and finally, the encounter with the old man/woman as a personification of the Self. Guggenbühl-Craig presents all the stages of a rather orthodox individuation fantasy from a new angle which highlights their dark, destructive aspects. The paradox lies in the fact that, for him, individuation is not a continuous process, not even in spiral form. That is the mythologem of continual progress, which he dismisses as dangerous in *The Old Fool*. Rather, individuation describes the moments of connection between ego and Self. These moments are discontinuous and follow no fixed progression.

Guggenbühl-Craig is able to bring his readers into the lower depths in a way that does not cut them off from the Self, but opens the possibility of encounters in areas where they had not generally been sought. It is for this reason that these monographs emit an unmistakable spirit of optimism despite the pessimistic nature of the material that they explore.

AND PERVERSITY

"Only a psychologist of the Jungian school can grasp Freudian psychology," writes Guggenbühl-Craig (*Marriage*, p. 82). Freud's magnificent contribution to the understanding of human nature results essentially from his explorations of the separation between instinct and psyche. His focus is on the problems that individuals experience because of that separation. He describes the neurotic symptom as a compromise formation, which attempts to satisfy both instinctual demands and the need for repression resulting from human culture. At the same time, Freud views instinct, sexual instinct in particular, as the source of all that human beings experience as psychic energy. Guggenbühl-Craig picks up these ideas, turns one on its head and takes the other to the borders of new and fruitful territory.

Guggenbühl-Craig's inversion comes with the suggestion that one should regard sexuality not so much as the source of all psychological energy, but rather as a principal mode in which psyche expresses itself. In Freud's formulation, the life process would be a manifestation of sexual energy. Guggenbühl-

Craig asks instead, ". . . can the totality of sexuality be comprehended from the viewpoint of individuation . . . ?" (*Marriage*, p. 80). This reversal of ground provides a new opportunity to "grasp" Freud's theories. It allows Guggenbühl-Craig to see the description of sexual development as an imaginative metaphor for expressing the overall development of the human psyche.

From this perspective, one could say that Freud has presented the world with a new mythology. Its gods include orality, anality and genital organization in a pantheon ruled by an hypostatized sexual satisfaction. Freud, along with his followers, took his ideas literally, of course and not symbolically. In contrast, Guggenbühl-Craig argues that the sexual life of the psyche represents a living symbolic system. Its elements touch every level of human existence—body, soul and spirit. Its images stir, but remain mysterious. It expresses both the developments of individuation and the chronicities of psyche and flesh.

It was Freud's genius to "discover" the unconscious and to find a path to it. For Jungians, sadly, his discoveries were difficult to appreciate, at least as they concerned the contents of the unconscious, because of Freud's insistence on their literal, reductive and mechanistic nature. As a Jungian, Guggenbühl-Craig has found a way to deliteralize, to find a teleology and to see the spirit or meaning in Freud's mythology.

One may approach many questions of concern to Analytical Psychology through a "proper" reading of Freud. To take but one example, Guggenbühl-Craig says, "Psychotherapy is, in the last analysis, an erotic activity" (*Power*, p. 71). He does not mean by this that, through the transference, the analysand will attempt to work through an old need to achieve sexual union with a parent. He means, rather, that a connection with the Self becomes possible through an intense encounter between two human beings, including whatever sexual fantasies may be constellated.

Guggenbühl-Craig's treatment of the "polymorphously perverse child," is another instance of how his ideas radically invert those of Freud. For Freud, this term describes the pure, undifferentiated libido of the pre-acculturated individual. Psychological development means gradual limitation of the forms of sexual expression and harnessing it for the biological "normality" of reproduction. Proper maturation means the end of the polymorphous, perverse child. Guggenbühl-Craig, though, asks, "What is this polymorphous, perverse child if not the Self of Jungian Psychology, the symbol of the totality of the psyche, the divine core within us which contains everything, all the possibilities and opposites of our psyche?" (*Marriage*, p. 93). Psychological life flourishes in the diversity of sexual imagination and individuation must mean long life to the polymorphous child. Freedom of life in the realm of imagination is a great liberation. That which might be intensely problematic, even criminal, at one level, becomes the *prima materia* for individuation at another.

Here lies the seed of Guggenbühl-Craig's significant contribution to the understanding of the psyche. Implicit in his writings is the recognition that the separation of instinct and psyche is not only an existential source of neurosis. It is also the opportunity for the unnatural and thus perverse work of a conscious individuation. A description of Guggenbühl-Craig's radical discussion of the perversions best illustrates this point. In his conclusion of *The Old Fool and the Corruption of Myth*, he uses the images of speech and dress as examples. There is another, darker, mythologem of age, which is not so harmless as these. It is that of the dirty, i.e., lecherous, old man. Although Guggenbühl-Craig does not discuss it, the image of he dirty old man personifies one of his concerns. The dirty old man is the obverse side of the polymorphous perverse child. What they share is perversity, in one case that of the young and not yet formed, in the other that of the old and rigidified.

Freud observed that perversion is the opposite of neurosis. He meant that if one lived out a perverse inclination, rather than repressing it, the neurotic symptom as a compromise between instinctual and super-ego demands would be neither necessary nor likely. Clearly, both the perverse and the neurotic are, in his view, pathological. The judgment of pathology, however, hands on the assumption of a firm attachment between sexuality and reproduction or "biological normality." Perversion is pathological because its aim is clearly non-reproductive. Similarly, neurosis is pathological, because its result is a deflection of sexuality into symptom, e.g., hysteria.

For Guggenbühl-Craig, the situation is quite different. Liberating sexuality from reproduction and representing it as a mythology of individuation, has the effect of negating the idea of "normal" sexuality. Like the individuation it can betoken, human sexuality also becomes unnatural and perversity, in fantasy at least, is freed from the onus of being only aberrational. One can allow sexuality to carry psyche as much as does the bizarre dream image. The ego is able to approach the perverse fantasy not with fear and repulsion, but in a spirit of honest inquiry.

The same holds true for neurosis. One might regard the neurotic symptom as an outer manifestation of the tension between conflicting and irreconcilable energies. The earlier discussion has already shown that, for Guggenbühl-Craig, this is the same conflict than can lead to psychological development. A major source of this conflict, of course, is the relative freedom from instinctual constraints enjoyed by the imagination. Yet, the subjective experience of the relative autonomy of imagination is essential for consciousness and, to go even further, is a defining characteristic of the human being. It is what makes individuation possible.

The separation between instinct and imagination, then, makes neurosis, perversion and individuation all fundamental possibilities for the human being. Guggenbühl-Craig addresses the interplay of all three phenomena through the images of *Eros* and *Thanatos* (the destructive shadow). The connection of individuation and *Eros* has already been discussed. In *Eros on Crutches*, Guggenbühl-Craig establishes the relationship between psychopathy and *Thanatos*. What, then, of neurosis? If ". . . completeness is fulfilled through incompleteness" (*Eros*, p. 25), then one might ask what does remain incomplete in Guggenbühl-Craig's theory? As an answer, one may recall an old Greek idea. It was said that *Eros* had two brothers, *Thanatos* and *Phobos* (fear). The relationship between fear and neurosis is self-evident and completes the pattern: *Eros* — Individuation; *Thanatos* — Psychopathy; *Phobos* — Neurosis.

Indeed, the perspective of fear would be a way of approaching many of the issues discussed throughout

Guggenbühl-Craig's writings. It is a major factor in the archetypal relationships he addresses in *Power*. Fear of his illness grips the patient and finds a reflection in his fear of the physician. The student fears ignorance and his teacher. The sinner fears divine retribution and his pastor as well. Fear has an intrinsic connection with power in the helping professions. Fear figures significantly in marital relationships and becomes almost a caricature in the image of the psychopath. Finally, as Guggenbühl-Craig makes explicit in *The Old Fool*, the fear of old age and its debilities has a real basis in universal human reality, not to mention the contempt and fear which the dirty old man evokes in all individuals.

"Psychology is mythology" (*Old Fool*, p. 35). If, as has been claimed, mythologems determine every individual, family and nation, it may be that they determine every body of work as well. In the case of Guggenbühl-Craig, the underlying divinities or archetypal images of his work are *Eros, Thanatos* and *Phobos*. The role of *Phobos*, the aspect of fear, receives the least attention of the three and, to turn a lack into a compliment (complement?), it may be that his special relationship to fear allows Guggenbühl-Craig to enter so deeply into what he calls, "the demonic depth of Jung's psychology" ("Jottings," p. 200).

POSTSCRIPT

From the Wrong Side is appearing in English as the author enters his eighth decade. It is an especially appropriate volume. The confluence of a lack of fear with the withdrawal of concern for the judgment of society, allows Guggenbühl-Craig to challenge a number of social and psychological assumptions. They are assumptions which individuals have taken so much for granted that they are generally beyond the pale of discussion. As one who has focused so much on the dark side of the psyche and, at the same time, has been such a progenitor of ideas and institutions, it is fitting that Guggenbühl-Craig should begin his discussion with a consideration of the children of the Devil!

—translated and edited by Gary V. Hartman

BIBLIOGRAPHY OF GUGGENBÜHL-CRAIG

"Analytic Rigidity and Ritual," *Spring 1972*, trans. Murray Stein (New York: New York Foundation for Analytical Psychology, 1972), pp. 34-42.

"The Archetype," *Proceedings of the 2nd Congress for Analytical Psychology*, ed. Adolf Guggenbühl-Craig (Basel: S. Karger Verlag, 1971).

"The Archetype of the Invalid and the Limits of Healing," *Spring, 1979* (Dallas: Spring Publications, 1979), pp. 29-41.

Erfahrungen Mit Gruppenpsychotherapie (Basel: S. Karger Verlag, 1956).

Eros on Crutches, trans. Gary V. Hartman (Dallas: Spring Publications, 1980).

"Has Analysis Failed as a Therapeutic Instrument: Analytical Rigidity and Ritual," trans. M. Stein, ed. J. Wheelwright. *Success and Failure in Analysis* (New York: Putnam & Sons, 1974), pp. 22-29.

"Jottings on the Jung Film, 'Matter of Heart,'" *Spring, 1983* (Dallas: Spring Publications, 1983), pp. 199-202.

Marriage — Dead or Alive, trans. Murray Stein (Dallas: Spring Publications, 1977).

"Medicine and Power: The Wounded Healer," *Harvest* (London: C. G. Jung Analytical Psychology Club, 1968).

"Must Analysis Fail Through Its Destructive Aspect," *Spring 1970*, trans. James Hillman (New York: The Analytical Psychology Club of New York, 1970), pp. 133-145.

The Old Fool and the Corruption of Myth, trans. Dorothea Wilson (Dallas: Spring Publications, 1991).

Power in the Helping Professions, trans. Myron Gubitz (Zürich: Spring Publications, 1971/82).

"Projections: Soul and Money," *Soul and Money* (Dallas: Spring Publications, 1982), pp. 83-89.

"The Psychotherapist's Shadow," *Reality of the Psyche*, trans. M. Cowan (New York: G. P. Putnam's Sons, 1974), pp. 247-257.

"We Are Such Stuff That Dreams Are Made Of," *Symbolic and Clinical Approaches in Practice and Theory*, eds. L. Zoja and Robert Hinshaw (Zürich: Daimon Verlag, 1986), pp. 365-369.

"Youth in Trouble and the Problem of Evil," *Andover Newton Quarterly*, vol. 57, 3. (Boston: Andover Newton Theological School, 1965), pp. 15-30.